Dictation Practice
Second Edition

B W Canning

Pitman

PITMAN BOOKS LIMITED
128 Long Acre, London WC2E 9AN

Associated Companies
Pitman Publishing Pty Ltd, Melbourne
Pitman Publishing New Zealand Ltd, Wellington

© Pitman Books Ltd, 1982

First edition 1975
Second edition 1982
Reprinted 1982, 1983

Isaac Pitman

Text set in 10/12 pt Linotron 202 Bembo
Printed and bound in Great Britain at The Pitman Press, Bath

ISBN 0 273 01803 5

PREFACE

This text, with the *Workbook Parts 1 and 2* and the pre-recorded dictation on cassette is intended to be used alongside *First Course* which explains the theory of the system.

Dictation Practice, second edition, comprises 21 sections. Section 1 corresponds with Units 1–5 of *First Course*; Section 2 is designed for use in class as soon as Unit 6 has been completed; Section 3 after Unit 7, and so on.

Each section of this book has a standard pattern: short form practice; phrases; dictation in three parts – (a) easy, (b) and (c) standard; theory checks and free dictation. All of these, except the theory checks and free dictation, are written in shorthand in the *Workbook*.

In each section, the theory checks consist of twenty words based on the theory taught to that point. As these are intended primarily as a check on students' progress, it is suggested that they be used by teachers as follows:

(a) Write up the words in longhand on a chalkboard and ask the students to write them in shorthand in their correct positions and with vowels inserted, allowing a two- or three-minute time limit.

(b) Write up the words in shorthand, read them to the students once, and ask the students to write them from the book, or from the chalkboard longhand, allowing a two-minute time limit.

(c) Give the outlines on an unlined chalkboard and ask the students to copy them, writing them in their correct position and inserting the vowels, allowing a two-minute time limit.

The passages of free dictation, each of about 100 words, do not appear in shorthand in *Dictation Practice Workbook Parts 1 and 2*. For the most part all shorthand used in the learning stage is better prepared by the reading approach to encourage a high standard of accurate shorthand writing. However, the challenge of writing from new material is motivating and interesting, and it is worthwhile to include

PREFACE

it in the programme from time to time. Care has been taken to ensure that most of the words used are those that the students have already seen and written before.

I believe that this book, the *Workbook Parts 1* and *2*, and the recorded material are an essential part of a beginners' course in Pitman 2000 Shorthand. By their use, students will rapidly become efficient shorthand writers, and speedy and accurate transcribers.

B W Canning 1982

CONTENTS

SECTION 1

Units 1 to 5
of Pitman 2000
First Course

1 SHORT FORM PRACTICE

(a)

it	for	manufactured	thanked
anything	the	but	do
thanks	are	yesterday	nothing
his	yours	we	have
too	ourselves	has	will
having	all	as	this
of	thanking	in	and
I	manufacturer	today	something
you	yourself	an	be
being	ours	with	manufactures

(b)

Short forms are included in sentences and the phrasing to be used is indicated by hyphens in **(b)** throughout this book.

  (i) I suppose we–have some of–your manufactures in–this depot. (**11**)

 (ii) Thank–you for manufacturing some of–the cases for–us. (**10**)

(iii) Will–you do something for–us today as–we–have to–go to–our manufacturers? (**15**)

(iv) In–this–case you–may–have to–go with–them today as they know nothing of–this. (**17**)

 (v) We–have manufactured all–the soap for–your customers and–we–have it for–you today. (**16**)

2 PHRASES

and the, to the, for the, but the, it is, it will be, will you, this is, with us, and you, in some cases, in some ways, you are, are you, as we have the, and as, as the, is the, we are, they are, we were, they were, I have the, we will, we will be, as we know the, as it is, I will be, it is the, is to, I know the, in his, to thank you, have they.

3 DICTATION

(a) Easy
In this case you may have to go to the / depot to get your things. (15)

Some of the rowing boats are red with yellow oars / and they are for our young customers. (17)

We are sailing to Rome and we will take with / us anything you may have for sale. We sail this / coming Wednesday. (22)

The road is being repaired, and this may delay you / for some hours. (13)

As you are going sailing in the boat today, take / some of the cakes with you and some of the / egg rolls, too. (23)

I will come to do the repair work today but / it may take some days to do it all in / a thorough way. (23)

Stow all the cases in the vessel and load them / in the space below the fore deck. Take care to / load them in the way we told you. (28)

This is a safe boat but it is slow. Will / you load it with some of the cases of soap / and take them to the lake for us? (28)

It is an error for you to go to the / railway depot as nothing will be sold today. The coal / is being sold this Monday. (25)

The red roses are named 'Dale Mason', and the yellow / roses are named 'Wedding Days'. We sold some yesterday and / with luck we will sell all we have today. (29)

(b) Standard
I know they will do the work of repairing the / doors with no errors. I have faith in them and / they will cope with anything they are faced with. (29)

This is a firm manufacturing tapes and they have a / world sale for them. They make them in any colour / and any length and they sell them in perspex cases / of a dozen. (33)

We have failed to take enough care of our customers / and it may be things will get worse in the / months to come. It is a lesson for us all. /

SECTION 1

We know the things we have to do for fame / in the coming months. (**44**)

Take a memo to Ray Mason. We are developing a / course for young nurses, and we have to get the / resources for them. We know Ray has enough and some / to spare and it is our purpose to come to / the depot to get the things to set up the / course in a month. (**54**)

I will come to your firm to get the cases / of soap and take them to the vessel 'Red Lake' / for loading. I have told the customs of this load / and I have paid for it. The 'Red Lake' will / be sailing this Thursday. Have you anything else to load? / (**50**)

(c) Standard

Have you space in your things to take some bales / of rope to the fair for us? We have two / bales stowed below this subway and you may care to / sell them for us in the fair. We will take / them up to your depot and load them for you / today. Customers owning boats will take the rope and you / will have no delay in selling the bales. / (**68**)

We have raised sums for the purpose of getting oats / and sago to aid the young folk and it will / come to you in bulk today. We have space located / in the vessel 'Red Rum' sailing this month. We will / get all this to you in cases for loading. (**49**)

Stay in the vessel. We will come to you today / with the oak doors and boards and we will stow / them below the decks. Sail to the bay and go / to the Tug Boat pub. Tell them you have the / things in the vessel. They will come with you to / get them and pay you for them. (**57**)

We have no resources of coal in the depot to / aid you, but we will get some. We have customers / with coal in Lake Dado and they will sell us / enough for you for a month and sail it to / you. It is said they will have it for you / in two days, and they will tell you the date / for loading it today. Mail them a sum today, too. / It will be safe for you to do this. (**79**)

Tell them we have a sum for them. We have / no way of getting it to them, and you may / tell them to come to the Cape for it. We / will be in the base all day, and they will / do well to come for the pay this Monday. We / sold all they manufactured in two days. (**57**)

4 THEORY CHECKS

naming	lessons	swung	fame
senseless	voted	yellow	slow
course	errors	mailed	debts
railway	Wednesday	borough	Thursday
suppose	colouring	memento	raises

5 FREE DICTATION

In the months to come they will work in a / thorough way to do the repairs to the depot they / were supposed to do in May. We are setting a / goal for doing all this, and we are paying our / work force for the work. Our sales rose, though we / have some customers failing to pay in Lake Dado. For / getting our manufactures to our customers, we have to thank / both railway and airways boards for our fame. Our sales / of gates and doors rose and we have no manufacturing / delays to tell you of. Things are developing well for / us. (**102**)

SECTION 2

Unit 6
of Pitman 2000
First Course

1 SHORT FORM PRACTICE

(a)

could	would	think	thinks
will	in	you	hours
any	this	manufactures	your
its	with	being	is
thanked	yesterday	doing	two

that	thinking	thing	thank
to	a	having	has
manufacturing	I	all	but
we	are	yours	manufacture
yourself	ourselves	our	the

(b)

(i) We–think–you–could manufacture some things for–us this month. (**11**)

(ii) You–wrote that–it–would–be enough for–us to–come to–the port. (**14**)

(iii) I–think it–is yours and–they–think it–is ours, but–we–will–have to–let–you–know. (**19**)

(iv) As–it–is some way to–the port, I–think–we–may take–the road to–the lake. (**18**)

(v) Would–you think–that this–is–the way to get to the port today? (**14**)

2 PHRASES

Let you know, we were, I think it is, we think you are, it would have,

5

to let you know, we could, that is the, you could, this is the, all that is, they were, I know that, would you, let us have, let us know.

3 DICTATION

(a) Easy

We think you may be expected to take notes of / the two-day course in export sales, and as you / are slow we will get Derek to do them for / you. (**31**)

We will let you know the result of the course / but it may take some days for us to do / this as we are working in the port. (**28**)

We will take the coats that you manufactured and export / them, but we will have to have some of low / weight for our customers in Wales. Will you cut them / for us and get them to our depot in Exmouth / in a month? (**43**)

We have all the support we expected for the report / we wrote that we spoke of yesterday. We think the / effect will be to get us enough votes to sway / the result our way. Supposing this is the case, we / will, in two months, be exporting coal and I think / we will become famous for it. Our customers have faith / in us, and our work force will support the course / we are taking. (**73**)

(b) Standard

Some of those sailing in the vessel that came in / to port have left things in it, such as notes, / cases and photos. Would you go to the port and / get them for us? We will pay all your fares / and any sums you may have to pay as well. / You will have to pay customs and some port rates / too. Would you let us have your support in this? / You may have some delay in the port in getting / the things, but we will pay you for waiting. (**89**)

A case of gold is located in the lake. We / have to get that gold, and the way we could / do it is to sail in the boat 'Lake Belle' / with a bale of rope kept for the purpose in / the depot, and set a course for the Cape. We / will have to select those to come with us with / care. We will have to take experts and have the / lake swept with weighted nets roped to the boat to / locate the case of gold. Some of them have swum / in the lake and know it well. It is up / to us to think of a method to get it. / Supposing we locate the gold, they will go below to / rope the case. Though we may take some days, our / aim is to save that gold. (**136**)

SECTION 2

(c) Standard

We manufacture and sell coats and capes in all weights / and colours for export. Some of them, we make in / suede. We take care in the cut and make-up / of our coats. This, and our thorough methods of selecting / the colours, is the base for our work and for / the results we get. It is your purpose, we are / told, to take some of them for your customers. You / are safe to do this. Our customers stay with us. / Have you a note of the low rates we let / sellers of our manufactures have? Bonus rates may be paid / too—something for all our customers to aim for! (**109**)

Sir, As we said yesterday, you have paid for all / the maize and oats that we sent you. Your error / is in thinking that the cakes of soap are paid / for too. We could let you have the bonus we / spoke of yesterday but you will have to pay the / debt to get it. Delay in paying for the cakes / of soap this month will result in the bonus being / cut. We are forced to do this as we have / to make a report to our Board. Pay in a / sum for this today less the bonus that you may / deduct. That makes sense and is the fair thing to / do. Yours, (**112**)

4 THEORY CHECKS

selected	swear	mason	Monday
notes	met	debate	late
seldom	lesson	length	resulting
erode	resources	vessel	weighted
road	slate	spoke	court

5 FREE DICTATION

We have sent you a memo noting the sum today, / and we have paid the manufacturers for the gates and / doors they let us have in May. Our customers have / sold all the things they selected, but as the debt / stays unpaid, we will be forced to raise a sum / in a month to pay the bonuses to our work / force. The expected result of having to raise this sum / will be to raise our rates for repairs and some / manufactures. We have to make a report to the Board / but, except for this, things could be worse for us. / (**100**)

SECTION 3

Unit 7
of Pitman 2000
First Course

1 SHORT FORM PRACTICE

(a)

shall	which	had	on
would	could	thinks	that
thinking	of	do	all
dollar	large	in	with
and	it	nothing	this
have	as	our	manufacturing
two	something	ourselves	doing
anything	be	for	thanking
yours	an	to	any
the	will	yesterday	thanked

(b)

(i) We–shall all get a large–sum today in dollars. (**10**)

(ii) Is–this something that–will go on–the page today? (**10**)

(iii) I–shall–be with–you on–Monday for an hour and–I–will come with a cheque for a large sum. (**21**)

(iv) Would–you let–us–have some dollars to pay for the manufactures? (**12**)

(v) Yesterday I–had a large case of things that I–had to–take to–the export fair. (**17**)

2 PHRASES

I shall, I shall be, we shall, we shall be, which is, which are, which will, on which, on the, on this, which were, which we have, I had, they had, we had, which you, which will, which will be, which may be, we shall have, large sum.

8

SECTION 3

3 DICTATION

(a) Easy

I shall let you have a cheque for the coats / on Monday. Will you fetch them on the same day / too? You could show them to your customers on Wednesday / and, as it is so cold, we think they will / purchase some of the coats. (**45**)

Yesterday you sent to us the budget for your estate / and we have noted on page two that you will / be paying less in rates. You may save, too, in / making some changes in your methods of paying debts. James / Dale thinks such a saving may be effected, and I / shall let you have a note on this. (**58**)

It is expected that the changes that we shall make / in your methods of manufacture will save you a large / sum and will raise your sales to your customers. Our / research shows that they will have the effect of raising / your export sales, too. This is a result of the / changes in the exchange rates that are going our way. / (**60**)

Having read the pages which you selected for us, we / support all you say in your report. You will have / to rush your manufactures of luggage but doing this will, / as you say, raise your sales. Tell the Board of / the changes that it is your purpose to make. (**49**)

(b) Standard

Our notes show that the repairs to your estate fence / were effected in May and the debt to us for / the work is unpaid. Will you let us have a / cheque for this work on Wednesday? We are searching for / the names of the customers you told us to get / in touch with and we shall let you have a / report on them, though it may be delayed for some / days. (**71**)

Some Dutch customers will be coming to stay with us / for a month so it is up to us to / take care of them. They will be coming in a / jet and they will be met in the airport. It / is up to you to do this for us, so / take the coach to the airport and fetch them to / the depot. We sent them notes of things we expected / they would care to do. As this report shows, they / have selected some of them. They have chosen to stay / in the Low Vale Motel and we shall take them / to lunch the day they come. (**106**)

It is Judge James's birthday on Monday. We know that / the judge is old but much respected for his sage / and expert words. Judge James will be staying on the / bench for some months yet. (**35**)

SECTION 3

(c) Standard
We are going to take all of our work force / on the boat for a day. The old may care / to stay on the shore in the sun and air. / Some will search for shells on the edge of the / lake. Some will make sketches and take photos, and those / young enough will take buckets and spades. All of them / will escape work for a day. (**66**)

We have read the essay you wrote on 'Ways of / Raising Export Sales', and it is so expert and thorough / that we are making space for it in the report / to the Board for the month. Will you check the / pages sent to you with this note and let us / know of any changes you may care to make? Would / you mail the pages to us on Thursday? We could / fetch them for you on Wednesday and thus save you / work. Let us know which way you have chosen. (**89**)

Some of the pages of this old tome are uncut / and some have errors in them. Will you check them / for us? We were searching for the tome for a / month but it is well worth it. We located it / on Wednesday in an oak case below the surface of / the edge of the road to the port, and we / dug up the old tome safe and untouched. The third / Earl of Essex owned it and kept it safe for / us in this way. It is worth a large sum. / (**90**)

4 THEORY

method	remote	shut	jet
yet	suspect	much	jade
expected	shape	ages	yell
report	shed	budgets	nurses
chess	sowing	research	customer

5 FREE DICTATION

Some of our customers are slow in paying debts. Sales / are low, but they are having to pay large sums / in wages. The result is that we are failing to / get the dollars we expected and so we delay paying / our debts, too. We shall have to report to the / Board on this and tell them that the repairs they / expect us to do will have to wait. We think / we may expect a change in a month, maybe two. / Our manufacturers of suede coats on a large scale will raise the rate of exports and so our guess is / that we shall leave no debts unpaid in May. (**109**)

SECTION 4

Unit 8
of Pitman 2000
First Course

1 SHORT FORM PRACTICE

(a)

ought	also	although	had
could	owe	shall	large
think	that	owes	on
always	thinking	which	owing
tomorrow	would	owed	dollar

for	being	his	manufactures
today	oh	a	anything
I	as	something	the
yourself	thanks	but	manufacturer
with	will	ours	yesterday

(b)

(i) I–think–we ought always to–let them have something to–do. (**12**)

(ii) Although–we also have some debts to pay we–shall make a large sum. (**14**)

(iii) We–shall pay them all–the sums we owe them tomorrow. (**11**)

(iv) Could–you tell them that–we–think our customer has some dollars for–them? (**14**)

(v) They also said that–they–had no cash although they know they owe–us for–the manufactures. (**17**)

2 PHRASES

It was, it was not, it is not, we were not, they were not, we shall not, which is not, customs charges, some charge, customs forms, bank forms, such forms, which are the forms, that this charge, this form, our charges, your charges, we shall form, or two, could not.

11

3 DICTATION

(a) Easy

We bought some works of art at the market yesterday, / and we shall be taking them to the shop at / Port Road to sell them to our customers. We expect / to make a large sum in cash on some of / the things we purchased such as watches and gold necklaces. / They were all part of a job lot that we / bought 'for a song' as the market was packing up / for the day. (**73**)

The road passes the farm, but you will have to / park your car and walk a long way along a / path to get to it. The oats are all in / sacks, so I think you ought to take a barrow / with you in the car and take it along the / path to load the sacks. You will have to pay / for the oats so we have sent you enough cash / for you to do this. Tom will let you have / the cash tomorrow. (**83**)

We shall not be coming to your shop tomorrow as / we shall be at the docks for the day, but / we have asked Tom to come and do the odd / jobs for you. We are ashamed that we shall be / absent because we had said that we would be with / you, but we have no way of escaping this job / at the docks. We have to go to the customs / and pay our customs charges to get some packing cases / loaded with our manufactures which are stowed in the sheds / at the docks. The customs forms say that we have / to take them all away tomorrow or pay a large / sum in taxes. (**113**)

(b) Standard

We wrote to you a day or two ago on / the changes in the law affecting the sale of manufactures. / The changes have yet to go to the courts but / we are told that, although some may oppose them, they / will be passed. Our lawyers have sent us some reports / on the changes which we shall have to note with / care. We think that we shall have to expect some / losses as a result of making repairs and adapting our / cars because of this law which will be in force / on the fourth Saturday in March, and that date is / not far off is it? We shall have to act / today to do all the work that is called for. / (**120**)

In March we wrote a report on managing large estates. / In that report we showed in the part that dealt / with research that some methods would pay and some would / not. The report met with much support and we are / told that some farms in the north, in which such / methods are working today, are making large sums. They have / left the bad old farming ways and are taking up / the methods of raising oats, maize, and potatoes that we / showed in the report would work. A result of this / is that the Estate Farming Gazette has asked us to / let them have the passages of the report for the / May Gazette. (112)

(c) Standard

The docks at the port are not well kept. The / roads are bad and some of the sheds in which / manufactures for exports are kept are unsafe. For months we / have urged the Dock Board to act and we have / repaired some of the dock gates, but the Board says / it has no cash for the work and the banks / have no resources to let them have any. Yet the / Board has today voted a large sum to erect workshops / in the docks. To delay the repairs is wrong but / we have faith that the Board will change the budget / and let us have the cash to get on with / the work. (112)

We have a range of packs of soap and boxes / of talcum for sale at the market shop tomorrow. A / customer owed us a debt, and to pay us sold / them to us as a job lot. Yet, except for / two cases of talcum, they are all perfect. The packs / of soap are in a range of pastel colours and / bear a famous name. They will sell well and we / expect to make a large sum though they will be / sold to our customers at a fair rate. We shall / mail you a cheque on Wednesday for your share of / a third of the sum we take tomorrow less the / sum you owe for a third of the purchase. (119)

4 THEORY CHECKS

chopped	smaller	car	bat
passing	laws	laughed	pad
catch	losses	arts	ball
guarded	luggage	balances	postal
opposed	passages	Thursday	charges

5 FREE DICTATION

We are attaching a note of all the sums you / owe us and we would ask you to pay this / debt this month. We know that your sales force had / bad luck with your exports of gates and padlocks to / Morocco, but we also know that you may call / on the resources of cash at the bank, and we / think you ought to call on such resources to pay / us the sums you owe. We have paid our customers / for the manufactures we sold you, and we think you / ought to attempt to raise the cash to pay us. / We suspect that you may be failing to pay because / of your bad luck in the export market. **(118)**

SECTION 5

Unit 9
of Pitman 2000
First Course

1 SHORT FORM PRACTICE

(a)

who	largely	owed	could
ought	are	although	dollar
owing	also	shall	think
always	owes	tomorrow	that
which	of	had	would
thinking	owe	is	oh
it	and	anything	able to
today	of	to	your
do	in	large	nothing
something	for	all	thanking

(b)

(i) Who-has a place for-the things that-were manufactured in-this works? (**13**)

(ii) They-have said that-they will-be-able-to pay-the sum they owe-us. (**15**)

(iii) We-shall-be with-you tomorrow, but who-will take care of-the shop? (**14**)

(iv) Such things are largely manufactured in-this part of-the world. (**11**)

(v) Today we-think we-shall-be-able-to support the Reds although they-are playing away. (**16**)

2 PHRASES

who is, who will, who are the, unable to, who has, would you,

15

with us, which is, which is the, we were not, claim forms, customs charges, local charges, sample forms, we are unable to, who is the.

3 DICTATION

(a) Easy

We shall go to the Clock Cafe for lunch today. / Joseph will pay for us all, and we shall have / raw vegetable salad with cold lamb and potatoes. Although the / Clock Cafe is small, it is a pleasant place. They / have the plates marked with the Russell coat of arms / and the tables are of old oak. Both the plates / and the tables belong to Tom Russell, who is the / son of an earl, and it is Tom who manages / the cafe so well. (**84**)

The Old Palace was sold in the autumn along with / all the effects of the Russells, and it was Tom / who bought the things that are on show in the / Clock Cafe. They also have some etched glasses and carpets / in colours that you are unable to get today. I / think we shall pass a pleasant hour or two in / the Clock Cafe. (**63**)

Sirs, We enclose our cheque which settles our debt to / you for the samples of glasses that we purchased in / March. We think that we also owe you for the / rail charges on the cases of bottles of port that / were sent to us on the railway a month ago. / Will you let us have a note of any charges / we owe? We have sent back the customs forms you / asked us for, and we are glad to despatch to / you today the plates and cups you asked to borrow. / (**90**)

(b) Standard

I have to tell you that on Saturday a small / bomb exploded among the cargo on the 'Red Rose' which / was in dock on that day. All those who were / aboard are safe and got ashore in small boats or / along the gangways. The cargo blazed for some hours, and / the port was closed all day on Sunday. The vessel / is safe, but we know nothing yet of any damage / or of the loss of cargo. We shall let you / have the facts in a telex message on Thursday. (**87**)

Jack Johnson is a person who gets a wage for / doing jobs of all sorts and working well at anything / that is asked for. For example, such jobs as repairing / the walls of the chapel in the church or in / adapting the shape of some old cart or barrow for / which a farmer has a purpose. Jack also makes coconut / matting and coloured rugs or will make you a set / of oak chairs and a table. In the local pub / they always say, "Call in Jack Johnson for any repair / jobs." **(91)**

(c) Standard
Sirs, We think that the barrels of tallow and the / casks of wax you are waiting for will come in / the sailing boat 'Sun Ray', a ketch that will get / in on Saturday. We have had customs forms for them / with a note of the dock charges that you will / have to pay and the forms are enclosed. We were / told at the docks that the ketch is expected on / Thursday, so we will have our barge at the dock / gates waiting for the ketch, and we will load all / the barrels and casks for you and fetch them ashore. / May we ask you to have your carts waiting on / the dock to collect them on Saturday. **(117)**

Something I have always thought of purchasing, but so far / I have not, is a globe. As a map of / the world that shows exact shapes a globe is unsurpassed. / It is also a pleasant object to gaze at with / its wealth of colour and it adds a warmth to / any space in which it is placed. **(57)**

4 THEORY CHECKS

glow	pledge	settled	tables
example	blazes	bottles	satchel
circle	total	angle	labels
black	model	arable	places
local	paddle	closed	glassware

5 FREE DICTATION

We have sent off to you today some samples of / our range of cups and saucers and you may select / any of them for your market. They are packed and / waiting in the depot to be loaded and despatched to / you on the same day as your note of those / you have chosen comes in to our works. Although we / had expected low export sales with this range, it is / selling well in all the large markets of the world / that take our tableware. In March, our catalogue will be / sent to all our customers. We have added your name / to our mailing and we shall let you have two / catalogues. Supposing that two are not enough for your purposes, / let us know and we will forward to you an / ample package of catalogues for you to arrange for a / local mailing to your customers. **(145)**

17

SECTION 6

Unit 10
of Pitman 2000
First Course

1 SHORT FORM PRACTICE

(a)

should	who	able to	tomorrow
largely	without	owes	also
ought	owe	influence	owed
always	although	which	influenced
influencing	shall	on	had

dollar	that	thanks	something
having	could	nothing	this
thinking	yesterday	think	several
would	of	but	thinks
influences	will	ourselves	all

(b)

  (i) We-are largely without cash at-this-time and-we-have-no influence to-get any. (**16**)
 (ii) Several of-the large manufacturers who-are waiting in-the bank are unable-to get any dollars. (**17**)
(iii) I-think-we-shall-have to-make several changes tomorrow and-we-know-that anything may influence change. (**18**)
 (iv) Several of-those-who-are without influence ought to-make an attempt to-get elected tomorrow. (**16**)
  (v) Although they-are always attempting to influence things, they largely fail and-they-are unable-to effect any changes. (**19**)

2 PHRASES

I am, I was, I will, I got, I refer, I came, I expect, I go, I may, I played, at times, at some time, at the same time, for some time, it should be, who is, it was not, it should not be, you should, you should not be, our charge, your charges, some forms, several forms, not yet, we shall not be, it would not be, all that is, let us have.

3 DICTATION

(a) Easy

Some of us have said that the time has come / to oppose the changes in the law that affect local / rights to make bye-laws. Those rights were bestowed on / us a long time ago and we think that they / should be kept today. We rely on you to support / us in the attempt to check those who are aiming / to make the changes in the law. We ask you / to sign the enclosed form and let us have it / back by Thursday. **(83)**

We were delighted to know that you had decided to / purchase all the plates, glasses and table-cloths for your / cafes at our shops. You are making a wise choice. / We are glad to accept the terms you ask as / to the method of paying for them, and we note / that you will make a saving for paying cash as / long as the total sum is paid in four months. / We note that you would like to have all the / items in your cafes by March, and you may rely / on us to arrange this for you. They will arrive / on time. We have asked our buyer to call on / you on the date named to settle with you the / times and dates of despatch to your cafes. **(128)**

Jack Blake is designing a range of textiles that we / shall be manufacturing. We are employing Jack Blake, who is / famous for his textile designs, because we are aiming at / a rising world market, and we expect to get a / large share of it as a result of his work. / We have sent samples of the designs available so far / to some selected customers in several parts of the world, / and we are awaiting replies. **(75)**

(b) Standard

We have not yet despatched the supplies of glasses and / table-ware that you asked us for because of a / 'go-slow' in the docks. Some of the smaller items / on the attached note are being mailed to you tomorrow, / but the bulk of the supplies will stay in the / sheds on the dock because we have no way of / getting at them without antagonising the dock work force. A / report in the paper says that the go-slow may / be settled in a day or two and we will / let you know which day we are able to load / your supplies. **(102)**

SECTION 6

We are manufacturers of toys and models which we make / in metal alloys. We employ no lead in the making / of our toys. Except for those marked with a red / arrow, supplies of all the items in the enclosed catalogue / are available for despatch. Our toys are supplied at charges / not matched by any manufacturer in the market at this / time, yet they are all at the top of the / range. We have boxed some samples which we ask you / to accept with our thanks for your call. (**88**)

(c) Standard

We have to face rising customs charges on our exports / in some parts of the world. At the same time / we are having to cope with a falling-off in / supplies of some of the alloys that we employ in / manufacturing our range of small metal items. We are relying / on supplies of the alloys arriving in our works some / time this month, so although we shall have some losses / to cope with because of the delay and the raised / customs charges, we shall be able to supply all our / customers who are able to wait for a month or / so. (**101**)

A job has come up today that calls for a / person who will repair the fences, walls and gates of / a large estate which is sited on the shores of / the lake. You would also be caring for the cattle / for an hour or two a day and that is / work that I know you enjoy. Apply on the job / form that I am enclosing. I will write a reference / for you. (**72**)

4 THEORY CHECKS

applied	night	census	employee
climb	choicest	arrives	oilwell
tight	rejoicing	mileage	enjoyable
silence	unavoidable	exercises	vital
success	clockwork	itemise	supple

5 FREE DICTATION

In the four months to which this report relates we / have had a rise in the charges for the supplies / arriving at our works for manufacture and also a wages / rise for our employees. This was settled to take effect / in March. We shall have to pass on some of / this to our customers and that is unavoidable. At the / same time I am glad to tell you that export / sales are up. We also expect to sell large numbers / of our light alloy rakes, spades and cutting blades to / customers in the world markets. (**95**)

SECTION 7

Unit 11
of Pitman 2000
First Course

1 SHORT FORM PRACTICE

(a)

immediate	without	able to	almost
who	influences	largest	influencing
thinks	immediately	on	owes
should	which	influenced	first
several	largely	ought	always
tomorrow	that	it	the
had	yesterday	of	for
also	would	and	a
nothing	thinking	any	this
owing	could	something	with

(b)

  (i) The largest of-the cases should–be loaded first, I–think. (**11**)

 (ii) Our immediate aim is–to ask who–is able-to come to–the fair. (**14**)

(iii) Send–us immediately, by–the first post, the largest samples that–you have. (**13**)

(iv) We–think we–shall-be-able-to influence almost all of–them, although several of–them have–not–yet arrived. (**20**)

 (v) Should–we go on without–them as–we–are late and–as almost all of–us have large packs? (**19**)

2 PHRASES

at first, first–class, for the first time, as fast as, just as, I came, I was, I placed the, I wrote, I expect, at times, at some time, at the same time, for some time, who is, who will, who are, they are, they were, on the, but the, it should not be, I expected, I may, I refer, I am, take us.

21

SECTION 7

3 DICTATION

(a) Easy

We lost the largest part of our stocks in the / fire at our depot in Chester Place. It will take / us a long time to get back to normal. We / are asking our customers to bear with us for a / time and to accept a small share of such stocks / as we have. We rely on them for support at / this time, and we think that most of them will / let us have it. We shall aim to supply our / best customers first and to buy some stocks in the / market. In this way we may be able to cope / for a month or two. By that time we shall / have doubled our manufactures. (**114**)

Thank you for sending us the play entitled 'Way of / Life' which you wrote for our next stage show. Several / of our best girls have read it and it is / much liked. Some change of plot is suggested in the / third act and changes in the dialogue, too, in some / places, but the play is exciting with wide scope for / acting and it has thought and charm. We have decided / to stage the play in March, and we expect it / will be a first-class success. We are glad to / enclose our cheque, and we will call you in to / advise us on selecting the cast for the play. (**109**)

(b) Standard

In the next day or two we shall be sending / our revised catalogue by post to some of our customers. / Most of our manufactures are of textiles and clothing and / we think that the styles and designs in the catalogue / will catch on immediately. We have large stocks available and / samples of the types of wear we have made will / be on the stands at the Textile Show which will / start in March in Leicester. It will be a first / class show, and we suggest that you write in for / a show card which will entitle you to a lunch / we shall be glad to supply. (**106**)

The largest estate in this part is owned by the / Wests who settled in Low Vale a long time ago, / though at first they resided in the north. We are / told that the Wests were rewarded with the Low Vale / estate for supporting the state in the attempts made to / stop the raiding for cattle that was going on at / that time. It was largely forest and marsh, but the / Wests worked at it, adding to the estate by purchase, / and step by step they changed most of it to / arable. It was rare in those times for persons who / owned estates to stay on them. They liked going off / to war. But the famous Master of Low Vale, Jack / West, who was a scholar and a person who loved / the estate with its

22

SECTION 7

meadows and forests, added to the / wealth of the Wests by encouraging the latest farming methods. / (**150**)

(c) Standard

Sir, Thank you for your cheque for the sum stated / and for the stamps you enclosed. You are right in / thinking that we employ experts in Hong Kong stamps. They / wrote a report on the items you sent us and / this is attached. The tests they applied show that two / of the stamps are fakes but they are rare fakes / and worth a large sum should you desire to sell / them. We will let you know the exact sum that / we are willing to pay for them. We shall be / glad to have your cheque for the cost of the / report some time. Yours, (**104**)

In cold climates the best way of saving large sums / is to double-glaze. This is a job in which / the first time is the last time so it is / worth doing well. Our double-glazing is the best and / although our charges are not as low as some, you / get the costs back in a short time. Our method / is devised to let in air on warm days but / shut it off on days of ice and snow. We / enclose some notes and suggested ways in which the costs / may be settled. (**93**)

4 THEORY CHECKS

stocks	cost	access	settle
next	caused	science	cycling
most	madam	deny	stated
bestow	standing	explore	cluster
stairway	pester	cable	monster

5 FREE DICTATION

In the last two months, we have had to face / a sharp fall in the sales of glass bottles and / at the same time a rise in the charges for / despatching the bottles to our customers. The fall in the / sale of bottles was the result of the fall in / the sales of ale and lemonade, showing the effects of / the local taxes that started last March. We think that / this fall will last for a month or two, but / that sales will rise in May as customers become accustomed / to the taxes. We shall cope with the despatch rates / largely by an immediate purchase of estate cars to supply / customers ourselves with the stocks they buy. (**117**)

SECTION 8

Unit 12
of Pitman 2000
First Course

1 SHORT FORM PRACTICE

(a)

dear	influence	immediately	trade
should	larger	largely	largest
toward	immediate	according	towards
without	large	who	according to
particular	trading	particulars	trader
able to	too	thinks	able to
yours	accord	almost	thinking
will	several	first	hour
influences	without	we	yourself
two	who	thanked	but
ought	also	although	think
always	owe	tomorrow	that
shall	which	owes	would
on	had	could	owing
owed	I	ourselves	dollar

(b)
- (i) According-to Jack Foster, we also have particulars of-trade in-several large stores. (**14**)
- (ii) Some of-the larger firms have-sent particulars of-trade in almost all-the markets in which they sell. (**19**)
- (iii) They ask-us to-let them have particulars of all our stocks immediately. (**13**)
- (iv) At-first we ought, according-to our sales manager, to-try to influence them to-trade with-us. (**18**)
- (v) We-were-the first to-trade without asking for immediate credit. (**11**)

24

SECTION 8

2 PHRASES

yours faithfully, yours sincerely, I regret, I regard, this company, your company, oil company, at first, for the first time, Dear Sir, at some time, at the same time, Dear Madam, with us, I am unable to, for us, at present, this is, this was, as long as, I regret the, low prices, Paper Co. Ltd., should be able to.

3 DICTATION

(a) Easy

Dear Sirs, At present prices we prefer to buy supplies / of rice in small lots as we think that in / September or October world prices will fall. We propose adding / to our stocks of rice in November and December, so / we will ask you to get in touch with us / at that time, letting us know of the lots you / may have for sale at the time of writing. Thank / you for the samples of cocoa. This is a strong / seller and we shall be glad to have four chests / which we shall collect and load on our trucks at / your depot. Yours faithfully, (**104**)

Dear Sir, I regret that you should have had such / trouble with the changes in the programme of the Trade / Fair. The changes were made without my knowing although I / had told my staff that any changes might well double / the cost of the programmes. I am, at this stage, / prepared to accept the revised price, and I am glad / to know that you may yet manage to send the / programmes off to this address on the first date I / had suggested to you. Yours faithfully, (**86**)

Because we have a much larger stand at the Trade / Fair this time, we shall be able to demonstrate the / correct way to operate our word processor. We are expecting / large numbers to come to the stand, many for the / first time and we are demonstrating on the hour, several / times a day. (**53**)

(b) Standard

Dear Sir, We are glad to support your research project / on changes in taste. You are correct in thinking that / less ale is bought today and that the sales of / cider and lager are rising all the time. But such / sales may last for a short time, and they are / much affected by changes in taxes. We suggest that you / should wait for some time and watch the sales of / all such items for a month or two. According to / our experts, the market has not yet settled. Yours faithfully, / (**90**)

SECTION 8

Dear Madam, In answer to your call yesterday the enclosed / report states that our metal shelves and brackets are tested / at the depot for strength and that all items which / fail the tests are rejected. Both weight and stress are / applied in this test, as described in the enclosed paper, / and as long as the brackets are fastened according to / the method we suggest, you may load the shelves with / any weight of normal stock. Yours faithfully, (**77**)

(c) Standard
Nursing calls for patience and thoroughness and the boys as / well as girls who follow nursing courses are respected and / admired by us all because we know that they will / be performing a job that could be vital to the / well-being of us all at some time in our / lives. (**51**)

Dear Sirs, In October, for the first time, the branch / of our store in Long Road will be selling our / famous products. In the first month we shall be selling / them at low prices and so we enclose our catalogue / with a card which entitles you to buy at those / prices. We shall be glad to come to your shop / to demonstrate some of our products should you be unable / to go to Long Road yourself. Yours faithfully, (**78**)

Dear Sir, We note that you have not yet paid / for the supplies of paper to your branches for the / months September to December. Particulars of the charges for the / paper supplies are enclosed. We think the fact that you / have not yet paid may be because of postal problems / a month ago. May we ask you to let us / have a cheque for the charges immediately as we have / to settle with our suppliers at the end of this / month. Yours faithfully, (**83**)

4 THEORY CHECKS

prices	grapes	darkness	sprang
prepared	surprising	occurrence	described
performance	regrettable	purchaser	preference
trial	entrusted	stretch	November
drawing	subscribe	straight	troublesome

5 FREE DICTATION

Copper is among the scarcer metals and because of that / its cost at any time is not low. At today's / prices, experts regard it as a dear but vital metal. / It is strong and lasts well so it is employed / in a number of ways in manufacturing processes. In particular, / pipes and vats for oils and fats are made of / it. Because it does not corrode, copper forms part of / most alloys. It occurs by itself or in ores, and / it is no problem to work it and shape it / to make wires and cables. It glows a pleasant yellow- / red colour. Copper in the soil is a source of / wealth. (**111**)

SECTION 9

Unit 13
of Pitman 2000
First Course

1 SHORT FORM PRACTICE

(a)

put	larger	thinking	toward
dear	to be	owed	largest
particulars	according to	putting	first
year	trade	towards	puts
Mrs	immediate	but	almost
accord	several	influenced	according
should	particular	ought	able to
without	who	immediately	although
influencing	owe	trading	tomorrow
owes	also	trader	influence

(b)

(i) This year we-are putting a larger-sum into-the bank for Mrs. Peters. **(14)**

(ii) According–to-the rules particulars of-trade sales are to-be put in-the report this year. **(17)**

(iii) We-shall-be putting almost all of-these rules into effect immediately and-this-will influence several of-our customers. **(20)**

(iv) You-will-have to-do without particulars of-several items of-trade this year as-the bill has-to-be made up immediately. **(23)**

(v) Mrs. King will-be-the first to-be put on-the list for a stand-by ticket. **(17)**

2 PHRASES

in this, in this city, it is, to be able to, please let us have, is to be, has to be, if we, if we will, if we are, if you are, if you are able to, just as, your business, some business, larger business, in business, our company, this company, Paper Company Limited, at least, please let us know, I regret, yours faithfully, yours sincerely, Dear Madam.

3 DICTATION

(a) Easy

Dear Sirs, Will you please let us have particulars of / each of the items on your list that you claim / were damaged in transit? Without these particulars, we are unable / to check the packing in the depot, and we wish / to settle your claim immediately. It may be that the / cause of the damage was the way the goods were / dealt with by the railway and we need to know / the facts to claim for any such loss. Yours faithfully, / (80)

Farms in the locality supply us with salads and vegetables / daily and they are packed and dispatched to our customers / on the same day as we receive them. This is / the way we are able to build up our sales / which this year are the largest we have had. Our / items of food are the best available in this city, / and we have built up our trade on the simple / principle of always selling the best. Our aim is always / to satisfy our customers. (**84**)

Dear Madam, We have received the two books that were / sent to you in error and we apologise for the / mistake. We are enclosing our revised invoice and a cheque / for the money you paid to send the books back. / We are also enclosing a leaflet showing particulars of books / you will be able to purchase in July at much / lower prices. The leaflet is published monthly and we have / put your name and address on our list of customers. / As you know, it is necessary to choose four books / each year to keep your name on our list. Yours / truly, (**101**)

(b) Standard

The policy of this business, which has several branches in / your area, is to sell a wide range of electronic / goods at the lowest possible prices. We are able to / do this because we manufacture all our goods and we / sell them ourselves in shops that we own. They are / not available to the retail trade. The result is that / we save money which is immediately passed on to our / customers in lower prices. Yet each item we sell is / the best in the trade. Our illustrated catalogue in colour / is sent to you without charge. If you study it / with care, the truth of our claims will be obvious / to you. (**112**)

An office is a place in which you may have / to work for a long time each week. For that / reason it should be a pleasant place with plenty of / light and air, and good seating adapted to the needs / of its users. Some business firms have seen clearly that / it is a mistake to save money on office fittings / and they have succeeded in creating offices that are almost / ideal for those who work in them. They have thick / carpets, the walls are in soothing pastel shades, and they / have ample space for each person to move and work / in. (**101**)

(c) Standard
Dear Mrs Kelly, I am pleased to know that you / are able to assist us by working on the statistics / of people living in your area. It will be necessary / for us to know first the total number of people / in the area including all those who are now employed, / and in a separate group those unemployed. We should like / you to classify the employed persons in these categories; first, / those in the primary stage of manufacture such as extracting / ores or making basic supplies for the next stage of / manufacture like steel rods or wood planks. The next will / be those who manufacture goods for sale; and the third / will be services, this group being split into two, namely / transport services and the rest. As you will see, you / will finish up with six groups in all. The booklet / enclosed will assist you by showing you the methods to / be used, and the way to classify people into the / various groups. Yours sincerely, (**164**)

A basic problem of typing is that if you aim / to increase your speed the number of mistakes you make / will rise. If you aim at typing without errors, your / speed will fall. To type fast yet without error is / not easy. To succeed in both aims, daily practice is / needed, but the practice time should be split so that / you aim first at speed without much regard being paid / to errors. At the end of a period of some / minutes, change the goal and aim at faultless typing. In / business and in office work, we have to try to / type both correctly and speedily. It is not easy to / do this. (**112**)

4 THEORY CHECKS

sizes	audio	killer	poodle
physical	policies	availability	industrial

succeeding	inevitable	simply	indicated
family	meals	July	clearly
medium	keeping	February	delicacy

5 FREE DICTATION

Dear Sir, Thank you for calling at the office today / to inform us that your name does not appear on / the voting register in this area. We have checked all / the details you supplied on the Registry Form and they / are all correct. It seems that a mistake was made / in this office at the time you changed your postal / vote to a vote by the ballot box in the / usual way. We apologise for the error, and we are / pleased to inform you that this is to be put / right immediately. Please fill in the enclosed form and post / it back to us in the envelope supplied. No stamp / is necessary. Yours faithfully, (**114**)

SECTION 10

Unit 14

1 SHORT FORM PRACTICE

(a)

how	dear	according	immediate
put	subject	Mrs	largest
to be	year	subjects	first
trade	larger	particular	subjecting
subjected	towards	almost	should

it	and	of	you
putting	accord	particulars	puts
anything	in	with	all
something	for	have	being
I	this	thanks	according to

(b)
  (i) How-much will I-have to pay for doing this-subject this year? (**13**)
 (ii) She-is-the best in-this-subject in New-York according-to Mrs James. (**14**)
(iii) If-we do-this we-shall-be subjected to attacks in-the papers by-the trade. (**16**)
 (iv) Which subjects are-you going to study first in-your course this year? (**13**)
  (v) We-shall send them our thanks immediately for-all-the trade they-have put in-the way of-our sales people this year. (**23**)

2 PHRASES AND INTERSECTIONS

how much, this subject, in this subject, in these subjects, New York,

32

in New York, are you, our business, your charges, some forms, entry forms, bank charges, Excel Company Limited, I thank you, I think you, ought to be, yours truly, this is, for us, by us, for the first time, at the same time, no doubt, we have no doubt, first class, as fast as, just as.

3 DICTATION

(a) Easy

Dear Sir, You will no doubt be proud to know, / now that you are back in this country, that on / Tuesday at the Royal South Show, your cows came third / in the individual tests of the output of milk for / the year. Still better, your entry for the ploughing came / first and so did your dogs in the sheepdog trials. / So you will have two valuable gold cups for a / year and a few small money prizes, too. We are / all delighted about the results. Yours sincerely, (**87**)

Dear Mr Trent, We shall be able to put up / five of your guests in single rooms at the Tower / Motel in South Avenue for the two nights you specify / in April. Each of the rooms has a shower and / we should be glad if you would ask each guest / to collect two bath towels on arriving. We are assuming / that you will be paying, as you regularly do, by / cheque. Please note that our new business title is "Tower / Motels Company Limited". Yours truly, (**85**)

Our reviewer writes: 'This book is the best I have / read on this subject. It presents a clear and accurate / view of the newspaper world as it is today and / the writers argue the case for bringing in new methods / to save the less fortunate papers which at present are / having a struggle to survive'. (**55**)

(b) Standard

Dear Mrs Powell, The value of the securities you asked / us to look at is, in the view of our / experts, at a peak. We suggest that now is the / time to allow us to put them on the market / for you. We think you should invest the proceeds in / a few good new stocks which present an opportunity for / us to secure a larger revenue for you at this / time. We think it is a fortunate time for you / to have approached us as we have no doubt that / the prospects for making money are good during the next / month or two. Please let us know your wishes. Yours / faithfully, (**111**)

SECTION 10

Dear Madam, A large cottage in a first-class state / of repair and with all fixtures included will come on / to the market soon. It is situated on the south / side of the avenue and the city is about two / miles away. At present it is owned and occupied by / a lecturer, but she will be leaving in a month / as she has a new post to go to in / Australia. We have no doubt that it would suit you. / Would you care to view it? Please call us at / this office to let us know. Yours truly, (**98**)

(c) Standard

We are unfortunate this year because, although we took each / opportunity to increase our market, and our sales both in / volume and in money terms rose, the cost of oil / and transport was so great during the period that we / now have less cash available to invest. We could have / saved money by laying off some of our workers, but / this we refused to do. On this subject our views / and our policy are clear. We are not in business / to add to the number of unemployed. We have a / duty to each individual who works for us and we / shall carry it out. (**104**)

Have you noticed how lifeless things sometimes take on life, / with the idea of making your day unpleasant, it would / seem? The tie that always ties so easily refuses to / do so. The soap leaps out of your grasp and / careers across the room. The dress that you hung up / ready to wear has moved to a place out of / your sight. The bed stubs your toes as you walk / past and the mat slides away as you step on / it. You stretch your arm and your blouse tears. Have / we any way of checking the malevolence towards us of / such objects? I think not. The thing to do is / to put up with it. The next day all will / be well, you will see. (**125**)

4 THEORY CHECKS

presume	mixture	country	Irish
outside	circulate	pursue	outlaw
loud	rescued	separate	dual
queue	proud	venue	rhyme
graduate	refusal	beauty	video

5 FREE DICTATION

Now that your video recording set is installed and working /

34

correctly, we suggest that you should have it valued and / insured as a separate item immediately. We are glad that / you have decided to take out our Service Policy for / a year because this will ensure that any fault which / may develop will be put right and any spare part / needed will be supplied straight away. Please note that we / are allowed to install a video set subject to the / purchaser agreeing that any recording made is strictly for the / use of the purchaser and his family. Will you please / fill in, sign, and send back to us the enclosed / form which deals with this subject. **(116)**

SECTION 11

Unit 15
of Pitman 2000
First Course

1 SHORT FORM PRACTICE

(a)

how	for	particular	largely
which	subject	influences	although
who	any	subjecting	putting
are	put	several	subjected
have	dear	without	tomorrow

had	always	but	manufacturing
also	anything	we	on
shall	thinks	yesterday	nothing
could	thanks	our	of
that	has	yours	it

(b)

(i) I-think-he-has a particular interest in-those-subjects which-will-be of help to-him. (**17**)

(ii) He-will talk about several of-these-subjects tomorrow as-he always does. (**13**)

(iii) Have-you any influence with him to-get him to-come tomorrow? (**12**)

(iv) Although he-is largely to-blame for all-this, it-is-not for-us to-raise-the subject. (**18**)

(v) If-we-have to-take him on our staff, does he-know anything about manufacturing? (**15**)

(vi) Yesterday we-sent him our thanks and also asked him if-he-could come tomorrow. (**15**)

2 PHRASES

he, he is, he has, he was, he will be, as he, as he is, if he, if he will, if he

36

will be, if he is, if he has, I think he, I think he is, I think he will, I think he will be, I think he will be able to, I hope, we hope, we hope you will be able to, we hope that he is, I hope that he is, at the time, at some time, at the same time, I know that he will, I hope you will be able to, I know that he is.

3 DICTATION

(a) Easy

We have a large garage at the side of the / hotel and here we have parking space for many cars. / If you could let us know how many cars will / be coming bringing guests to the lunch we could hold / a whole area of the parking space for them. We / charge a small parking fee for which we issue a / ticket, but tickets may be redeemed for cash in the / hotel bar. Will you please let us know about this / soon? (**81**)

Mr Tom Lee will be coming tomorrow to address the / Club on the subject 'Housing and Homes', and he will / be arriving for lunch. He is a highly expert and / famous speaker, and we are expecting the Club Hall to / be full so we have hired loudspeakers. If the Hall / is full, members may also hear his talk in the / lounge, should they wish to do so. Several extra helpers / will be on duty in the bar. Mr Lee has / promised to adhere closely to the programme times so we / shall, as usual, close the doors of the hall as / soon as he is ready to speak. If you wish / to hear him, you must come early. (**117**)

This holiday spot is in a healthy area. It has / a firm beach of yellow sand with hills on both / sides of a bay. Below the cape at the south / of the bay lies a small harbour of great beauty / and interest. The sea water is crystal clear all the / year. The sun is hot in July and August, but / the heat is not too great. Sail boards and small / sailing yachts may be hired. The bay is so safe / that nobody is likely to come to any harm. The / hotels are first-class but you may also hire houses / or beach homes for the period of your holiday and / cater for yourselves. If you come you are assured of / a happy time. (**123**)

(b) Standard

A large business has built up in the last few / years in hiring out goods. Today in many countries, it / is possible to hire almost anything, such as household items / like cooking utensils and glasses as well as things to / help with the housework like carpet shampooers, electric tools and / drills. If you need it, you may also hire the / whole package for a huge party with marquees and bar, / a buffet hot or cold, and the people to supply / the service to go with it. I have heard that / in North America you may hire a racehorse for the / day with all the right clothes for yourself to enable / you to appear at the track as its proud possessor! **(120)**

Dear Miss Long, Thank you for letting me know about / Margaret Lee. I was able to meet her at her / hotel and take her to lunch. We discussed the leasehold / property on the Harbour Highway, but I think it will / be hard for us to purchase the lease because just / now a local law prohibits the use of any houses / in the area for business purposes. All the same, my / lawyer has heard that this law may be held not / to apply to us since our business is to raise / money for charity not to make money for ourselves, and / he is looking into the subject for us. I was / delighted to meet such a charming lady as Margaret Lee. / Did you know, for example, that she is an expert / astrologer and casts horoscopes? Did you know that a few / years ago she had a hole in the heart, but / that this was put right and she is now in / full health? She is fortunate to have both high ability / and beauty, too. Yours sincerely, **(175)**

(c) Standard
Dear Sirs, We hope you will be able to let / us know some time this week if Mr Hall will / be calling on us soon to talk about the new / products that we have bought for this season. I know / that he is extremely busy at this time, but if / he is able to call in here to see us, / we shall appreciate it. He knows so much about our / market and our customers that it would be much better, / as no doubt you will agree, if he were to / come to us instead of anybody else. We are unable / to get in touch with him ourselves, so we hope / we may rely on you to ask him to fit / in a call at any time up to next Tuesday. / We are starting the display and sale of the new / products on Wednesday. Yours truly, **(145)**

4 THEORY CHECKS

high	perhaps	unhappy	hillside
hat	harvest	warehouse	harmony
wholesome	whom	disinherit	horsepower
heartless	harmonious	neighbourhood	helping
whose	haulage	harbour	hurried

5 FREE DICTATION

Sleep is necessary to all of us. We could not / stay healthy without it. In all parts of the world / it is the custom to sleep in some of the / hours of darkness and to stay awake in the daylight / hours. Yet sleep is largely habit. Some medical authorities now / take the view that many people sleep too much. It / has become the usual thing to regard it as right / to sleep for a third of each day, yet it / is not hard to make do with much less. The / medical authorities say that young people may need as much / sleep as this but that most people, and in particular / old people, would be in better health if they slept / less and took regular daily exercise. Many famous people such / as Caesar and Madame Curie slept for as little as / four or five hours each day. **(146)**

SECTION 12

Unit 16
of Pitman 2000
First Course

1 SHORT FORM PRACTICE

(a)

nothing	to be	of	his
for	put	in	without
have	had	larger	on
be	thing	too	all
subject	any	that	will

according to	Mrs	almost	able to
thanked	who	first	ought
how	dear	should	owes
subjected	trade	subjecting	also
year	immediately	largely	shall

(b)

(i) Will-you be trading with any of-them in-the new year, do-you think? (**15**)

(ii) According-to Mrs Day we-shall-be-able-to do a larger trade with-them now. (**16**)

(iii) Thank-you for putting your notes for-the-year on-this-subject in-the post yesterday. (**16**)

(iv) I-had almost nothing to say on-the subject, but some of-them spoke for hours. (**16**)

(v) He ought to-tell them how-much he owes to-us for-the success he-has had. (**17**)

2 PHRASES AND INTERSECTIONS

you will, you will not, I am, I am not, it will, it will not, it will not be, we will not, I will not be, business man, for the first time, would you, I thank you, this charge, we shall arrange, we are arranging, I am arranging, he has arranged.

3 DICTATION

(a) Easy
Dear Sirs, I have tried several times to reach you / by telephone, but I was told that the post office / had found a serious fault in a main telephone cable. / Since you asked for my opinion immediately, I am sending / this by express mail and messenger. My opinion is that / the settlement you propose in the dispute about the leasehold / property is absolutely legal and correct and that you are / making all the allowances possible. I think that you have / a strong case, and that the payments demanded are fair, / and that they will not be refused if we have / to go to court. Yours truly, (**106**)

Dear Mr Lane, I am sorry to tell you that / the payments you suggest for the settlement of your debt / to us are not sufficient to satisfy our Board. They / have asked me to say that they are ready to / make allowances for your problems at this time which are / well known in the trade. They will not, except as / a last resource, go to law yet they are ready / to go on supplying you with machine tools and lenses / so that you may carry on with your work if / you find that you are able to increase the amount / of your monthly payments by a tenth. This will lead / to a steady fall in the balance you owe us. / They will themselves bear all the insurance charges. We realise / that it will not be easy for you, but they / will not go on as at present to the detriment / of our business interests. Please let us know if you / are able to agree with this arrangement. Yours truly, (**169**)

(b) Standard
The way in which the memory works is indeed strange. / People will tell you that events occurring years and years / ago may be called to mind immediately with all the / clarity of a camera lens. Things that occurred yesterday or / a week ago may fade into oblivion. Not enough is / known about memory to be able to state the reasons / for its capricious behaviour though it often seems to work / to our detriment. We are clear though that we each / have several systems of memory such as a memory for / words and sounds, for things seen, and for movement. It / is also clear that we each have a short-term / recall which enables us to hold some fact for a / few moments such as a

telephone number, and during these / moments we are then able to dial that number. We / also have a long-term recall and things we remember / for a long time seem to be based on knowing / the meaning or of feeling deeply about them. **(168)**

Dear Mr Finney, We have examined the stones you sent / us, and we are pleased to tell you that they / are all genuine diamonds. Two of them are fine diamonds / and worth cutting and polishing as gems. The rest are / suitable for industrial use. We are arranging for the insurance / of the stones and will send them back to you / by air within a few days. Full details of weights / and present values are enclosed. Yours truly, **(77)**

(c) Standard
Dear Madam, Thank you for asking us to advise you / about your present investments in shares and unit trusts. We / are sure you will not mind waiting for our experts / to study the details you sent us. They will let / you have an opinion and you may rely on it / as being the best available. We shall also arrange to / send you details of the way in which you might / reinvest to get the income and security that you have / in mind. A statement of fees for the work is / enclosed. **(91)**

In his talk, the speaker said that in the past / the idea of an educated person was of an individual / who knew a lot and who could think but was / not taught to act or to exercise useful skills. Today / it is realised that people have to be educated to / earn a livelihood, to find out how to solve problems, / to make things and to be capable of playing a / useful and practical part in the society in which they / live. Today with hours of work steadily being reduced, a / third aspect was vital. We had to educate people to / enjoy life to the full as well. We had to / make allowance for the need to educate people to live / as satisfying a life outside working hours as within them. / **(130)**

4 THEORY CHECKS

alone	remain	mint	manpower
man	remains	document	manhood
often	romance	element	telephone
union	balance	settlement	sunshine
means	balances	garment	zone

SECTION 12

5 FREE DICTATION

Dear Sirs, We are sorry that the machine we installed / for you a few weeks ago has caused trouble. This / type of machine is usually highly efficient and reliable. By / the time you receive this, our workmen will have installed / the replacement machine, and Mr Lane will stay for two / days to ensure that it is working correctly. We have / found that the fault on the machine you sent back / arose because too much heat developed, and we think this / was caused by the excessive speed at which it was / operated. We are arranging to fit a speed checking device / on the machine so that it will not be possible / to operate it too fast. Yours faithfully, (**117**)

SECTION 13

Unit 17
of Pitman 2000
First Course

1 SHORT FORM PRACTICE

(a)

cannot	year	larger	putting
have	responsible	according	immediately
subject	Mrs	gentleman	how
put	subjected	particular	gentlemen
to be	dear	trade	almost
first	subjecting	subjects	puts
according to	toward	immediate	dear
responsibility	trades	putting	should
towards	without	influence	largest
several	influencing	accord	particulars

(b)

(i) I-cannot-be responsible for-any particulars on-that-subject for-this year or last-year. (**16**)

(ii) According-to this gentleman it-is our responsibility to-let them have-the particulars of-this year's trade immediately. (**19**)

(iii) We-have-the largest trade in tea with-this region but-we-cannot-see any-way to-make-it larger. (**20**)

(iv) It-is your responsibility, gentlemen, to-send them particulars of-this trade immediately. (**13**)

(v) Dear-Mrs Jones, We-have almost all of-the particulars on-this-subject and-we-hope to-let-you-have them soon. (**22**)

2 PHRASES

had not, do not, did not, you are, you are not, you will, you will not,

SECTION 13

I am, I am not, at once, it is, it is certain, I have been, we have been, have been, I had been, better than, our own, your own, we are not, they are not, I had not, I do not, I did not, I went, I want, we cannot, are not, you will not be, we can, I cannot.

3 DICTATION

(a) Easy

Dear Mrs Jones, Thank you for calling us. I am / sorry that I was not in the office at the / time, but I am writing immediately to let you know / that the results of this year's trading will be better / than last year's. You should receive a cheque in a / week or two, and I can tell you that it / will be for a much larger sum than you received / last year. We think it will be at least a / third up on last year. Yours sincerely, (**87**)

We have named our new cassette play-back the Music / Box. It uses silicon chips and the result of this / is that the music you listen to is so perfect / that it seems as though you are actually present and / sitting in the middle of a large orchestra. It has / no loudspeaker and you hear the music by plugging in / a light head-set which can be adjusted to your / own head. The sound is so lifelike that some of / our customers have been writing to us to say that / they think we should have called it the 'Magic Box' / because, they say, it is even better than hearing the / music live in a hall. (**115**)

On the eastern side of the town we still have / some houses that are not really fit for people to / live in. These are due to be pulled down this / year, and we have been working for the last two / years on plans to build our own council houses. It / is our responsibility to reduce our long housing list and / we must tackle the problem at once. (**67**)

(b) Standard

Dear Miss Brown, Thank you for your suggestion that we / should appoint an agent for our garden supplies in your / own area. We hope you will not be too disappointed / if we tell you that though we would like to / have an agent in your locality, we cannot do this / till we have a garden depot within a short distance. / This is an expense that we cannot take on at / this time as we have been setting up two such / depots in the western region. We hope to be moving / into your area in about two years time, and we / shall then appoint an agent. Yours truly, (**107**)

SECTION 13

Most people seem to enjoy dancing. Many people still like / the formal kind usually known as ballroom dancing. That type / has a long history and it remains as popular today / as it was a century ago, but modern disco and / 'pop' dancing, though it appeals mostly to the young and / vigorous, still has its fans among all ages and classes. / The rhythmic physical movement of the dance expresses joy and / art and its story began as far back as we / have any records. **(83)**

(c) Standard

In the last statement we sent to you with full / particulars of our trading in the period April to September, / we have now found certain errors for which we apologise. / Would you please accept the revised statement now enclosed? We / think that the following notes will make clear the changes / you will notice in the charges made. First we omitted / to credit you with the returns of damaged goods, and / this has now been put right. Then we had not / charged you for the boxes of ground rice, and you / will find this charge as item two in the new / statement. Lastly, we had not allowed you the agreed discount / on the goods despatched to you at the end of / October and you will notice that this discount is now / item four on the revised statement. The total balance, as / you will see, is much less than it was. We / hope to receive your cheque in settlement of the account / in the next four weeks. **(165)**

Fire, it is said, is a good servant but a / terrible master. We use the power of fire to help / us in many ways – to cook our food, to keep / us warm, to supply power for factory plant and machines. / As long as we can manage it and keep it / in check it is a good servant. But it is / unfortunate that so often fire takes on a force of / its own and then it becomes a destroyer. Then it / turns against us and we have to fight it to / protect our buildings and our lives. In each country of / the world, fire services are set up to guard us / against its ravages. Each year thousands of fires happen which / result in serious loss of life and property. The extent / of this loss may be seen in the returns of / the great insurance firms. Some recent examples are the deaths / of all the passengers in a ferry boat burned in / the Caribbean and of all the passengers in a Jumbo / jet which was gutted by fire as it came in / to land in Arabia. **(184)**

SECTION 13

4 THEORY CHECKS

plains	princes	second	torrent
between	spinster	want	handwriting
maintain	diligence	background	bonus
turnings	assistance	students	relevant
declined	happens	pound	importance

5 FREE DICTATION

Machines and electrical appliances of all kinds are now found / in most homes. One result of the great increase in / the number of home machines is that a service industry / has grown up to meet the need for servicing machines / and supplying spare parts. It cannot be expected that such / items as radios and washing machines, cassette players and vacuum / cleaners, will go on and on without something breaking or / something going wrong. So, it is important that at the / time these items are bought an agreement should also be / made for maintaining the item in good repair and for / servicing it at regular times during the year. (**108**)

SECTION 14

Unit 18
of Pitman 2000
First Course

1 SHORT FORM PRACTICE

(a)

particularly	putting	to be	immediate
gentleman	accordingly	year	largest
responsibility	gentlemen	Mrs	almost
cannot	trade	larger	first
how	responsible	towards	several
should	who	ought	which
influence	largely	that	on
influences	able to	owing	dollar
without	tomorrow	also	large
several	although	always	shall

(b)

(i) This year we-have a particularly large trade with several firms in dollar countries. (**14**)

(ii) We-cannot take-the responsibility without pay so accordingly we-are-not accepting the post. (**15**)

(iii) How-can we influence Mrs Jones who-is always particularly against our views? (**13**)

(iv) Are any of-the gentlemen here able-to suggest any immediate steps we-can take? (**15**)

(v) Several of-our largest customers are buying less and-we-are accordingly likely to-get less trade. (**17**)

(vi) This year we-hope to influence those-who owe-us money to pay largely in dollars. (**16**)

2 PHRASES

sales department, fire department, export department, how much, too

much, your business, local business, our charge, your charges, did
not, do not, had not, had been, better than, our own, your own, at
once, I am not, I cannot, we are not.

3 DICTATION

(a) Easy
Dear Sirs, May we remind you that the cheque we / asked you to send
in payment for the work we / did for you in June has still not been
sent. / We have telephoned you several times and this is the / third
time that we have written about it, but we / have had no reply. Please
explain the long delay for / which we know of no reason. Would you
ask your / accounts department to send us the cheque by the end / of
the week as the delay is causing us problems / in making payments
that are due to our own customers. / Yours truly, (**102**)

We have been visited by the Fire Department, as most / of you will
know, and they are not ready to / let us have the necessary safety
certificate until we have / made several changes. The points that have
to be put / right are, first, four new fire doors have to be / erected on
the top storey; second, the outside fire escapes / have to be strength-
ened and new metal steps fitted. Third, / up-to-date fire appliances
have to be bought and / set up in all offices. All these things have to /
be done at once, and so we shall have to / put up with some problems
of noise and movement during / a period of several weeks. (**115**)

As a result of good work by our Sales Department / we now have
several new and important customers in the / west region and it seems
likely that we shall add / to this number in a month or two. So we /
shall need a new salesman or saleswoman to take on / some of the
work in the region. If you wish / to apply for this post, please ask Mr
Downs for / the necessary form. (**73**)

(b) Standard
Our personnel department has recently issued a report asked for / by
the Board, the subject being the methods they use / to ensure that the
firm is correctly staffed, that no / instances of excessive staffing occur,
and that as far as / possible all members of staff are fully employed and
totally / involved in jobs that are exactly suited to them. They /
actually do this work by means of a monthly review. / At the end of
the year they then analyse the / staff needs for the next annual period
and the adjustments / that may have to be made. Announcements are

made of / any new posts and appointments according to the need. In / all cases departmental heads co-operate with the Personnel Department. (**119**)

It seems that several of the assignments for the coming / year will be for visits abroad. Plainly, some of our / staff are better fitted for such work. They have to / be physically strong and intellectually suitable for the work and / it is important to remember that they are not acting / for themselves or even for the department that sends them, / but they are responsible for the image of our firm / in the regions they visit. It is hardly necessary to / stress, then, that they should be chosen with care since / the appointments made will strongly influence the success of the / firm. They need to be totally involved in the job. / (**110**)

(c) Standard
Dear Jane, I am happy to be able to tell / you that the Board has agreed to the suggestion that / you go abroad for four weeks. A first-class apartment / will be found for you and all your living expenses / will be paid so that you will not have to / spend anything out of your own pocket. Also a bonus / of a fifth of your salary will be paid on / your return to this country. It is true that you / may feel lonely at times but we are certain that / you will do an excellent job for the firm and / hope that you will now be able to say 'yes'. / Yours sincerely, (**112**)

Recently a new monument has been erected to Leonardo da / Vinci in the Italian city of Milan. He was one / of the outstanding geniuses of history. He was not only / a celebrated artist (his Mona Lisa is world-famous) but / he was also far ahead of his time in mathematics / and in science. Among the things he invented were a / submarine, a paddle steamer and a mechanical saw. He stated / the laws of heat and light and studied optics and / gravity. His fame is as great today as it was / in his lifetime, five centuries ago. (**96**)

4 THEORY CHECKS

until	recently	experimentally	cheaply
only	unfortunately	instalment	weekly
annual	increasingly	announcements	wholly
analysis	exceedingly	disappoint	suddenly
unlikely	experiment	disappointment	mainly

5 FREE DICTATION

You are due to pay the first instalment on your / hire purchase of a washing machine on the first day / of June. The last payment will be made on the / first day of May, the total period being two years / with one payment each month. We suggest that you should / insure your purchase at once and we enclose a proposal / form for you to fill in. As you will see, / it is not only an insurance against loss or damage / but also includes the service needed to maintain the machine / for the whole period. The rates we charge are the / lowest in the business. **(104)**

SECTION 15

Unit 19
of Pitman 2000
First Course

1 SHORT FORM PRACTICE

(a)

knowledge	ought	also	responsibility
cannot	acknowledge	tomorrow	which
who	owe	particularly	on
gentleman	always	gentlemen	accordingly
largely	yesterday	owes	owing
shall	cannot	Mrs	influencing
had	acknowledgement	responsible	would
acknowledging	owed	according	gentlemen
larger	also	but	particular
two	influences	could	acknowledged

(b)

  (i) I-shall acknowledge his note tomorrow but I-cannot do it today. (**12**)
 (ii) You-will-require a knowledge of-trade particularly of-trade in-these areas. (**13**)
(iii) A gentleman who owes us some-money and accepts his responsibility will pay-us tomorrow. (**15**)
 (iv) We-shall make enquiries tomorrow and accordingly I-want you to-be responsible for-all calls. (**16**)
  (v) The knowledge that-he-has on-this-subject would-be largely wasted in-this job. (**15**)

2 PHRASES

we shall require, we have enquired, this enquiry, your requirements,

52

it will be required, legal requirements, anything required, we are, we are not, you are, you are not, they are, they are not, did not, do not, had not, I cannot, I want, it will, it will not, it will not be, it is, it is certain, at once, have been, had been, better than, our own, your own.

3 DICTATION

(a) Easy

Dear Miss Lee, We thank you for your enquiry. We / are pleased to tell you that the loose-leaf books / that you require are available in red or green bindings. / The paper is of first-class quality, and we have / stocks of off-white or pale lemon, both plain. Each / of these can be bought in wide-line ruled feint, / too. You know where our shop is. Why not call / on us when you come into town the next time? / We shall be pleased to show you our stocks and / to advise you what is best for your needs. Yours / sincerely, (**101**)

We think we have by far the finest stock of / language books in this city. We do not sell single / copies though, because our trade prices are so low. We / deal only with schools and colleges and we allow discounts / on all purchases. Particulars of these discounts are shown on / the enclosed list. You will notice how much you save / on large quantities, and we quote even lower prices for / quantities of a hundred and upwards. We have no doubt / that we can satisfy all your requirements. All the leading / titles are always in stock. When books not on our / own list may be required, we can obtain them within / a few days. Let us know what you need and / when you will call, and we will appoint one of / our sales staff to take care of you. (**138**)

(b) Standard

The English language has many points of interest about it. / For example, it is quite rich in monosyllables. When you / try to write a passage of one hundred words in / words of one syllable, you will not find it too / hard to do. A reader raises an interesting question. Why / is it that people do not seem to know when / to push a door or when to pull it? The / answer is that the two words are not unlike enough / for them to be distinguished easily at a quick glance. / So people push when they should pull. Have you noticed / that words beginning with the same sounds like *squeeze* and / *squash* and *squabble* mostly have somewhat unpleasant meanings, and that / words like *where, when, what, why* and *which* are all / question words? (**132**)

Dear Mr Jones, We have been told by Messrs Brown / and Dunne that you require at once a large quantity / of scrap metal and particularly of brass, bronze and zinc. / We have adequate stocks of all these metals today, and / we can quote prices that are better than any in / the area. Our price list is enclosed. If you will / let us know what you want and where and when / you wish it to be sent, we think it is / certain that we can supply you. We assume you will / want the scrap in block form. We have all the / equipment for this. Why not call at our depot and / examine our stocks? Yours truly, (**115**)

(c) Standard

Dear Sirs, We shall require by the end of June / a large quantity of insect killer both in liquid and / in powder form made up in metal aerosols. Can you / meet these requirements? If so, will you please quote prices / to include packing in wooden cases and transport to our / warehouse for quantities of a hundred cans per week. The / cases have to be strong enough to qualify for the / shipping rules for cargoes anywhere in the Middle East. Yours / truly, (**81**)

It may well be the cheapest in the long run / to buy articles of the highest quality you can afford. / They look better, they last much longer, and they are / better for the purpose. A quick bargain may often turn / out to be not a bargain at all. Shoes are / a case in point. When you require new shoes, then / make up your mind to buy the best. Adequate shoes / can be bought at a reasonable price, but shoes that / will still look good even when old cost a lot / yet the expense is certainly worth while. In the same / way, it pays to buy articles that will be expended / in fairly large quantities even if storing them is a / problem. Quite large amounts of money can be saved by / bulk buying. (**132**)

4 THEORY CHECKS

quota	requisite	anguish	nowhere
request	exquisite	squid	whale
inquest	quaint	square	wheeled
linguist	quarrel	bequeath	liquids
what	why	where	elsewhere

5 FREE DICTATION

Most people do not take as much exercise as they / should. They go by car when it would be better / for them to walk. They sit at home when a / quick bicycle ride for an hour each day would keep / them fit. Not many jobs in these days require much / physical work. We use our brains but not our muscle. / Yet we have to remember that the brain is itself / affected by our physical state. When we have oxygen in / the blood and we are healthy, then the brain works / faster and better. The sense of well-being and fitness / that comes as a result of daily exercise will amply / repay you for the trouble you take to make it / a regular routine. (**123**)

SECTION 16

Unit 20
of Pitman 2000
First Course

1 SHORT FORM PRACTICE

(a)

satisfactory	acknowledge	gentlemen	commercial
knowledge	together	more	from
particularly	responsible	altogether	subjects
cannot	gentleman	before	very
accordingly	there	how	put
their	Mrs	particular	acknowledging
to be	that	trade	towards
year	responsibility	before	according
commercially	acknowledged	influences	should
acknowledgement	larger	without	influenced

(b)

  (i) Our trade was very-much more satisfactory this year than before. (**11**)

 (ii) More commercial subjects together-with more English will-be taught this year. (**12**)

(iii) They-will-be-able-to get more of-their-requirements from-the commercial depot. (**14**)

 (iv) I-cannot take over their responsibility for our commercial success altogether. (**11**)

  (v) I-acknowledge that-their results are-no-more-than satisfactory, but-they-are very-much better-than before. (**18**)

2 PHRASES

very little, very much, I am very sorry, there is, there is no, there are, there are no, there are now, I acknowledge, more than, no more than, any more than, sooner than, I am, I will, I can, I agree, I trust, I refer, I go, I want, and there is no, but there is no, before me.

3 DICTATION

(a) Easy
Dear Frances, Do you happen to be free on Friday / next week? I know you have very little leisure these / days, but it would be such a pleasure for me / to take you out to lunch and then perhaps go / on to a film or a play. We have met / so infrequently lately that I almost forget the last time, / and yet we always enjoy ourselves when we do meet. / There is nothing I should like better than a day / out together. So look with favour on the offer and / say 'yes'. If Friday is not possible, what about the / following Thursday? Yours sincerely, **(104)**

We can offer you an immediate cover for your car / insurance whether you were insured with us before or not. / Our policies for business drivers with clean licenses are better / than any others that are available today and the cover / we offer is much more favourable and more extensive. The / particular virtue of our car insurance is that it rewards / the safe and accident-free driver. We do everything we / can to encourage safety on the roads. However, we have / to add that we are not interested in insuring any / driver who has been successfully prosecuted for any offences against / the highway acts. Our success as car insurance experts is / measured against your success as a safe car driver. **(119)**

(b) Standard
Deep in the valley, the river runs like a silver / ribbon shining in the summer sun. On its banks for / about three miles on either side are fertile plains where / are the farms and fruit trees that have very often / stood there for centuries. Some olive trees in this region / are known to be nearly a thousand years old. The / road and the rail track follow the river through the / valley. You are never far away from the murmur and / babble of the water as it slides past rocks and / bridges. Today the weather is good and the forecast is / that it will stay sunny for several days. We pass / the old stone tower where scholars from the university discovered / the remains of a former bronze age village and some / silver brooches that are now in the museum in Milan. / We shall endeavour to reach that great city by Friday. / **(150)**

SECTION 16

Dear Mr Freeman, We are frequently asked whether we have / on our list of speakers someone who can speak at / universities to young students whose knowledge of the grammar and / syntax of the language is less than it should be / because they were never taught these things at school. Your / name has been offered as one who is expert in / this field but who has a different manner of approach / to the subject. We hear that your aim is to / make the subject a pleasure to the students by using / visual and audio aids. If, when you look through the / enclosed brochures, you are interested in being a member of / our team of speakers we can offer you very favourable / terms. We forecast a rising pressure of demand for such / talks from junior members of the universities, and we advertise / in all the leading journals. Please get in touch with / us. Yours truly, (**153**)

(c) Standard

Dear Sirs, It was a pleasure to receive the silver / wine cups only three days from the date the coupons / were posted and this is to acknowledge their receipt. The / silver is of high quality and I now have them / in my display cabinet. I gather from the note you / enclosed that I still have a credit of a hundred / coupons. I now send a thousand more coupons and a / new form for the two books offered – 'Treasures of Africa' / and 'The Century Book of Verse'. Will you please supply / these in the hard blue covers as advertised. Yours faithfully, / (**100**)

Dear Sirs, You promised to deliver three books on leisure / arts and hobbies more than a month ago. Although I / have telephoned you and written twice on this subject they / still have not arrived. Do not now send the books. / I would sooner recover my money. It is clear that / my efforts to obtain the books have failed and I / will not suffer any more delay. I am not interested / to know whether the books are in stock or not. / Please send back my cheque or the cash by return / of post. Yours truly, (**94**)

4 THEORY CHECKS

difference	fertility	forget	beginner
government	moral	shrank	joiner
departmental	insurance	dinner	leverage
otherwise	discovery	overseas	mercy
pleasurable	freezing	banner	advertisement

SECTION 16

5 FREE DICTATION

There are two reasons for reading. Either we read to / find out the facts or we read for pleasure. Sometimes / these two reasons come together as, for example, when we / look up a word to discover its meaning and then / go on reading about other words and phrases because it / is all so interesting. There are some who would rather / read anything than nothing. If the only reading available is / a timetable or a list of the minerals of Africa / then they will read that. Whether we read as a / part of our studies or as a leisure enjoyment, there / is no doubt that reading enriches our lives. (**108**)

SECTION 17

Unit 21
of Pitman 2000
First Course

1 SHORT FORM PRACTICE

(a)

enlarge	very	influential	knowledge
satisfactory	enlarging	together	particularly
altogether	from	more	acknowledge
enlargement	commercial	there	enlarges
their	enlarger	thankful	responsible

influential	ought	although	on
gentleman	enlarged	owing	responsibility
how	owe	commercially	largely
subject	always	who	before
years	tomorrow	able to	also

(b)

(i) I-will-not enlarge on-this-subject but I-am thankful that-we-are-able-to end it. (**18**)

(ii) He-is very influential at-the Commercial Bank and-is at-present enlarging his influence. (**15**)

(iii) Their enlarger is very-good and-they-are especially good at enlargements from small photos. (**15**)

(iv) Although all-present knew-the subject I-could-not stop him enlarging on it at-length. (**16**)

(v) Her knowledge of-the commercial world makes her very influential on-the board. (**13**)

2 PHRASES

as early as, as early as possible, it is possible, it is not possible, it was possible, if possible, as soon as, as soon as possible, as soon as we are, as soon as we can, as soon as we know, as soon as they are, United States, United States of America, New York, this month, six months, next month, some months, several months, every month, each month, very little, very much, there is, more than.

3 DICTATION

(a) Easy
Dear Miss Russell, We hope it is possible for you / to come along to the General Knowledge Quiz that we / are holding on the first Friday in November and to / join the panel. There are special prizes donated to us / by the Commercial Bank, and the first prize is a / cheque and a weekend in Paris, France. Several more excellent / prizes are also offered. The Question Master will be Andrew / Marvel and the quiz will take place in the evening. / Tea and coffee will be available free before the start. / Please let us know as soon as possible whether you / will be able to come. Yours sincerely, (**107**)

Dear Madam, I will call in to see you as / soon as I return from Scotland, but my arrival back / home may be delayed. In the meantime, will you please / arrange travel to France for me in the usual way? / I have to travel on the first Saturday in October / and an official car is being sent by the French / naval department to pick me up at the airport. There / is no need for a hotel booking this time as / they have put a beautiful flat in the heart of / Paris at my disposal. The charges will be met by / cheque on my business account. Thank you. Yours truly, (**119**)

(b) Standard
We hope to begin a trek across East Africa next / month. This region of Africa is especially rich in beautiful / flowers, many of them quite marvellous in shape and colour. / On the face of it, one might think that because / the largest part of Africa is well known, it is / not possible to find new flowers. However, the fact is / that new ones are discovered every year and we hope / that we too will be fortunate enough to return with / some original species hitherto unknown. We have a powerful tracked / vehicle at our disposal, but we shall also travel on / foot and for a short distance by camel. (**108**)

As most of you will already know, the purchase of / new premises now has the approval of the Board. The / removal to the new premises will take place in three / stages, the first of which will take place in October. / The final stage is not possible until February. Management, then / support staff, and the Financial Department will move first. In / the second stage, which will take place as early as / possible in December, specialist machine staff will move. A brochure / which states full details of all aspects of the removal / will be issued to all members of staff this week. / It should be carefully studied and, when the time comes, / acted upon. Each step in this manual should be carried / out in sequence and as far as possible adhering to / the original plans. (**133**)

(c) Standard

A good supply of fresh pure water free from any / form of life harmful to its users is essential for / a civilised society. In most countries the supply of fresh / water is a first call on local and regional resources. / Some countries are fortunate in having ample rainfall. Others have / special problems in enlarging their water supplies to meet the / growing demands of industry and home users. Some partially meet / the demand by purifying and distilling sea water, but this / is not possible for some countries because of their financial / problems and the high capital cost in the initial stages. / Some cities, such as the capital of Saudi Arabia for / example, are located where they are solely because in that / spot there is an unfailing source of good water. (**129**)

Dear Jack, In a few months as soon as we / have our manufacturing plans ready, it will be necessary to / send over a team to New York. We need to / meet our American colleagues and to travel across the United / States of America to talk with the managers of factories / there. I am writing as early as possible to let / you know that the Board have decided that you should / lead this team. Your task will be to ensure that / the terms of the agreement are fulfilled by both parties; / mine will be to finalize the financial details. Nothing is / urgent now, but give the project some thought. Let us / meet in some peaceful spot away from the offices next / month to discuss it all. Yours sincerely, (**127**)

4 THEORY CHECKS

level	helpfulness	devil	civilians
harmful	penalty	cavalry	originality
animal	kennel	wasteful	manual
tunnel	canal	meaningful	impartially
channel	flexible	specialize	unofficial

5 FREE DICTATION

The amount of manual work that is done in the / world is still huge, but manual jobs are far fewer / than they were even a few years ago. This reduced / amount of manual work reflects the steady technical progress that / is going on everywhere, but particularly in more industrial countries. / Muscles are yielding to machines. Each month, machines can do / more jobs and they can do them very much faster, / too. Even so, it is unlikely that machines will ever / take over all manual work. There will always be work / in which the hands and brains of men and women / will be essential if certain jobs are to be well / done. **(111)**

SECTION 18

Unit 22
of Pitman 2000
First Course

1 SHORT FORM PRACTICE

(a)

difficult	together	commercial	responsibility
satisfactory	difficulty	knowledge	cannot
altogether	their	influential	accordingly
very	more	enlarged	thankful
before	from	particular	particularly

and	any	acknowledge	have
of	enlargement	with	something
should	anything	enlarging	our
to	all	for	difficulties
in	thanks	this	has

(b)

(i) It-is a particularly difficult job that-we-can only do satisfactorily together. (**13**)

(ii) Our responsibility is to-take on this difficult job for-we-have-the knowledge to-do it. (**17**)

(iii) I-am-very-sorry to-hear that-you-have had difficulties in-this-work. (**14**)

(iv) We-have-had a very-satisfactory year in-spite-of our early difficulties. (**13**)

(v) I-acknowledge that-it-is-difficult to-go from-your job to-this but it-will-be a much more influential post. (**22**)

2 PHRASES

out of, part of, in spite of, instead of, sort of, much of, set off, better

64

SECTION 18

off, take off, state of, state of things, copy of, rate of interest, you have, which have, who have, who have not, number of, member of, type of, lack of, advantage of, range of, which have not, instead of the, part of the, much of the city of,

3 DICTATION

(a) Easy
Dear Sir, Thank you for the rough proofs of my / report and for the copy of my original typing. As / you will see, I have divided the copy into paragraphs. / I am now returning the corrected proofs to you together / with some suggestions for the graphic design and artwork so / that it can be well displayed on the pages of / the magazine. Am I right in thinking that the next / step will be for you to send me more proofs / in which the report will be set up in page / form? I have not had very much experience of this / work and I want to do it well. Yours truly, (**110**)

Dear Miss Greaves, I have sold all the shares according / to your wishes and in spite of the dull state / of the market I managed to get good prices. The / total profit on the sale is, as the enclosed statement / shows, more than £3000. A cheque for £600 / is enclosed which is an advance that you / asked for of 20 per cent of the total. My / fees will amount to £200. I know that / you wish to divide what remains among various investments. As / soon as you have decided how this is to be / done, please let me know, and I will then see / to the rest of your requirements. Yours sincerely, (**118**)

(b) Standard
One of the great problems of city life is the / management of the traffic. The number of cars and vans, / buses and heavy trucks goes on increasing, and driving in / any large city can be both tiring and alarming. In / recent years efforts have been made to preserve some areas / of the cities for shoppers and to defend the city / against the car by keeping these areas free as shopping / precincts. Time and money are devoted to such schemes and / they deserve to succeed. The difficulty of providing enough parking / space is one more problem that has to be faced. / In some cities, streets are reserved for one-way traffic / with the advantage that in this way a steady flow / of traffic is achieved and there are few hold-ups. / Yet positive thinking is still required if the problems of / city traffic are to be solved. (**146**)

SECTION 18

You have already received part of the supplies requested by / your representative when he was here. I am very sorry / that we are still out of stock of photographic plates, / but we should definitely have them early next week. We / have 230 of the type of rolls / of film you wanted but some have defects so if / you approve we shall send 190 on / account and we hope to supply the rest within a / week. Last month we reserved some cameras for you. Please / let us know at once how many you will require. / (**100**)

(c) Standard

Today in most countries of the world the 24- / hour clock is in regular use especially for travel by / rail and air, and often in commercial firms, too. Some / people still have problems with this sort of time recording. / Midnight as '2400 hrs' does not exist. We / can write 2359 now, which is a / minute to midnight or 0001 hours which / is one minute into the next day. Notice that these / times are always shown by four figures and no stops / are necessary. In ordinary day-to-day use we generally / stick to the old way and we write 9.30 / a.m. or 3.50 p.m. though in speech / we often say 'half past nine' or 'ten minutes to / four' for these same times. (**135**)

The number of people in the world goes on rising / and each day there are about 200,000 more / mouths to feed. People die at about the rate of / 110 a minute, but they are being / born at over 240 a minute. At / this moment in the decade, the total number of people / in the world is about 4,400 million, / and at the end of the century it is likely / to be over 6,000 million. Seventy nine thousand million / people have lived since mankind first became a species. In / the English-speaking world the United States of America has / the largest number with about 220 million. / Nigeria has about 80 million and Great Britain about 59 / million. But the giants in this field are China / with about 840 million and India with / about 620 million. (**156**)

4 THEORY CHECKS

curve	prophesies	graft	brevity
drove	approve	inactive	pivot
raft	strive	restive	festivity
gift	cliffs	profit	relativity
achievement	cafe	profitable	doves

5 FREE DICTATION

You have noticed, I expect, that to achieve your aims / in this subject steady daily work is essential. You will / only advance in speed and knowledge by working at the / subject every day. Take a positive view. Make up your / mind that you will succeed, and that in itself will / take you a long way towards success. Is your writing / good? Use the shorthand in the workbooks as a model. / Are your outlines correct? We all make mistakes over outlines / now and then, but the more outlines you have tucked / away in your brain in that part of it labelled / 'automatic; ready for immediate use', the more you are likely / to become a successful writer. Remember also that writing of / any kind is only there to be read. If writing / cannot be read, then it is of no value. (**139**)

SECTION 19

Unit 23
of Pitman 2000
First Course

1 SHORT FORM PRACTICE

(a)

therefore	difficulty	together	commercial
there	wonderful	satisfactory	altogether
difficult	enlargement	wonderfully	knowledge
influential	thankful	very	January
more	before	from	commercially

difficulties	enlarge	doing	acknowledged
their	accordingly	itself	enlarges
acknowledging	thankful	its	enlarger
gentleman	enlarged	responsible	particularly
enlargement	acknowledge	responsibility	enlarging

(b)

  (i) I-think, therefore, that-we should-be thankful for a wonderfully satisfying year. (**13**)

 (ii) Our commercial venture began very-well in January but-there have-been some difficulties. (**14**)

(iii) Though-we-are influential in-this area, we should-not therefore think that-we-shall-have no difficulties. (**18**)

(iv) From-the report we-got an altogether more satisfactory knowledge-of some very difficult problems we-have to solve. (**19**)

 (v) In-the January issue we-had wonderful enlargements of pictures showing the peak before and-after-the volcano erupted. (**19**)

2 PHRASES

I have, I have been, I have been there, we have been there, I know, I

68

know there is, we know there is, I shall, I shall be there, we will be there, if there is, we think there is, some other means, in other ways, in other words, your order, their order, in her letter, for your letter, later than, lighter than, I can be, I can be there, for there.

3 DICTATION

(a) Easy

Dear Sirs, We thank you for your letter. You will / be glad to know that our sales force will be / there at the Modern Typewriter Show in January. We shall / be putting on display our new electric typewriter which has / the facility of correcting errors before they appear on the / typed line. All you have to do is to press / a cancel button and you are back again at the / last typed character that has actually been typed on the / paper. We think there is every chance that this typewriter, / which is of the 'golf ball' type, will rapidly come / to be very popular. We enclose a leaflet about this / very great advance in typewriter design. Yours faithfully, (**118**)

Dear Miss Featherstone, We have sent off today the duplicator / that you ordered in your letter of 14th January, and / we think there is a very good chance that it / will arrive two or three days earlier than we at / first said it would. This will give you the opportunity / to try it out and get used to it before / you have to demonstrate it on 3rd February. The pocket / recorder that you asked us to obtain for you has / been promised for 28th January. As soon as it / arrives we shall check it, and if there are no / difficulties and it works in a satisfactory way, we shall / dispatch it to you by road on the following day. / Yours truly, (**122**)

(b) Standard

Agriculture can be both a very profitable but also a / very risky activity. Many factors have to be taken into / account. The weather today can greatly affect the crop of / the future. Then there is the positive loss of or / damage to crops through disease or insects or natural disasters. / World events may easily interrupt the demand for certain crops / or even stop it altogether. Soya beans sell well all / over the world but the price may be very much / affected by the size of catches of anchovies off Peru, / because they are an alternative material used as the basis / of cattle feed. (**103**)

I understand that the builder of these houses will not / only install all the fixtures and fittings but will also / be responsible for all the furniture, too. This was included / in the original tender for the job. However, purchasers will / have the alternative of buying their own furniture. Having seen / three or four of the furnished houses, it is not / surprising to learn that more than a quarter of the / total number of houses to be built have already been / sold. The character and quality of the houses and of / their furniture and fittings is such as to ensure the / rapid sale of the remainder. We suggest you buy immediately. / (**110**)

(c) Standard
Dear Mr Proctor, I hope I may call on you / one afternoon later this month to discuss with you the / matter of the pictures that you have asked us to / put up for sale. Some of them are wonderful examples / of the work of painters who are very popular today. / It would be premature to estimate the total for the / sales but we think there is no doubt that it / will much exceed what you thought. We should like you, / therefore, to set a reserve price on some of the / less valuable pictures and we shall need your signature for / a number of documents. May we suggest that one of / our directors, Mr Paul Stiles, should call on you and / that we make an arrangement for an interview to be / televised about a week before the sale. This would involve / neither you nor ourselves in any expenditure. Yours sincerely, (**149**)

Somebody once said that it is always later than you / think, and we believe there is a thought here to / give us pause. We all tend to put off what / ought to be done now to some other time or / in other ways to defer the things we do not / wish to do and turn to another more attractive job / that is really not so urgent. It is the natural / thing to do, and is an aspect of human character. / But we must be stern with ourselves and make up / our minds to tackle all the tasks that face us / in the order of their priority. Who knows? By taking / this advice you might start a new chapter in your / life. (**121**)

4 THEORY CHECKS

enter	moderate	internal	surrender
mature	interrupt	unilateral	rafters
leather	interval	fritters	boarder
leader	aster	quarter	fixture
voter	entertain	remainder	adventure

5 FREE DICTATION

The history of stamps begins with the founder of modern / postal systems, Sir Rowland Hill, and with, perhaps, the most / famous of all stamps, the Penny Black of 1840. / Since that time the sender of a letter / has had to affix the small adhesive paper shape called / a stamp on to his letter as a token that / he has paid for its delivery. Tens of thousands of / different stamps have been designed all over the world. Design / requirements are that a stamp should use colour and words / to make it a clear symbol immediately understood; that it / should be so exactly drawn that it can be perfectly / printed and that if pictures are to be shown on / the stamp, they should relate in some-way to the / character or the history or the flora and fauna of / the country issuing the stamp. (**145**)

SECTION 20

Unit 24
of Pitman 2000
First Course

1 SHORT FORM PRACTICE

(a)

information	difficult	altogether	from
there	satisfaction	wonderfully	more
therefore	influential	satisfactory	before
wonderful	enlarger	difficulty	unsatisfactory
January	together	very	accordingly

commercial	from	their	who
should	commercially	influential	altogether
but	acknowledged	difficult	thankful
responsible	there	enlargement	particular
two	immediately	shall	enlarged

(b)
 (i) Thank-you for-the information in-your-letter of 7th January even though it-is unsatisfactory. (**16**)
 (ii) Any-information that-we-send-you is aimed to-give you satisfaction. (**12**)
 (iii) This book has unsatisfactory illustrations, but it-is full of wonderful information about-the Far East. (**16**)
 (iv) We-had more-than usual difficulty in getting the commercial information you asked for and it-is-not altogether satisfactory. (**20**)
 (v) The present-position is very unsatisfactory and-we should like-you, therefore, to-send-us more information about-the January sales. (**21**)

2 PHRASES

this corporation, large corporation, steel corporation, your attention, our attention, some attention, more attention, in other ways, some other business, if there is, if there is not, as we know there is, I shall be there, for your letter, later than, we believe there is, out of, in spite of, better off, take off, you have, who have not, immediate attention, these corporations.

3 DICTATION

(a) Easy

Dear Sir, We thank you for your letter and for / the information about the number of customers who have not / yet paid their January bills. You may rely on us / to act immediately on this information. Please note that we / have a success rate in the collection of debts of / more than 70 per cent. We charge 5 per cent / on the total sums actually collected plus a standard fee / of 20 dollars for each account on which we are / not successful. Yours truly, (**84**)

Most nations of the world have gone through a period / of inflation in the last twenty years, and the situation / in some countries has been sensational with inflation of 100 / per cent per year. What does this mean? It / means that each year the amount of money in circulation / has exceeded the production of goods and services. The relationship / is that when the proportion of money to goods rises / then prices will rise. The solution is, of course, either / to keep the levels of money and goods stationary or / to bring about a reduction in the supply of money, / or to create a situation in which more goods and / services can be produced. None of these solutions is easy / to bring about, and so inflation still goes on. (**129**)

(b) Standard

It is a mistake to think that good handwriting is / irrelevant to the situation today, and that it is unnecessary / to teach it in the traditional way. It is true / that most documents used in business today are typed or / printed, but writing is still widely used also. The truth / is that we have grown accustomed to accept immature and / illegible scrawls, and that people generally have become indifferent to / the art of writing. In the office, one has to / write with pen or pencil many times a day. Reports / and letters may be originated by dictation, but there is / still a large proportion that began as drafts written on / sheets of paper. Each secretary and receptionist also uses ordinary / writing on many occasions in the day. So instruction in / the art of writing clearly and quickly is in no / way irrelevant to office work. Nobody in business should be / indifferent in the matter of penmanship. (**156**)

SECTION 20

(c) Standard

Dear Miss Rhodes, Thank you for the final items of / information relating to your total earnings for the year. Our / position now is that we are ready to go ahead / on the taxation details for the year, but there are / still one or two decisions to be taken and one / or two items that may need alteration or modification. For / that reason, it will be necessary for you to call / in at the office for a discussion and for at / least one instruction to us that will need your attention. / For example, it is still not clear to us whether / you now hold independent ownership of the books and stationery / shop in the city centre or whether your parents retain / some rights in its operation. There are other additional points, / too. So will you call us as soon as possible / to let us know a time and date when we / may expect you? Yours sincerely, **(155)**

A main attraction this year will be the exhibition of / old books and documents that is being organized by the / National Arts Association in the City Hall under the direction / of Peter Jones. A fine collection is being assembled with / many items of distinction and exceptional beauty, many of which / will not have been seen in this country before. The / catalogue, already available at 50 dollars, is itself a work / of scholarship. Application forms for admission are also obtainable with / special days and low rates for educational visits. One section / of the exhibits will go up for auction at the / end of the exhibition. **(104)**

4 THEORY CHECKS

nation	physician	irresponsible	unnoticed
national	musician	irrational	unnatural
international	transition	immaterial	leadership
fashionable	accusation	immobilisation	chairmanship
moderation	succession	illegitimate	friendship

5 FREE DICTATION

It is natural that people should pay attention to fashion, / and try to make their selection of clothes the best / and most modern they can within their means. Clothes have / many functions and one of them is to attract admiration / and to satisfy self-esteem. The dedication of women to / following the dictates of fashion is not peculiar to them. /

74

Men are really in the same situation, only their fashions / change more slowly. In the past this was not the / position, and it was men's styles of dress that showed / the most variation and exaggeration. We have little information about / how the decisions to change are taken or why one / idea will be received with exceptional favour whereas another will / die unnoticed almost as soon as it appears. (**128**)

SECTION 21

Unit 25
of Pitman 2000
First Course

1 SHORT FORM PRACTICE

(a)

nevertheless	wonderfully	enlarging	very
their	notwithstanding	difficulty	more
therefore	difficult	information	before
January	influential	together	satisfaction
unsatisfactory	thankful	satisfactory	from

altogether	difficulties	trader	responsibility
accordingly	acknowledgement	there	cannot
commercial	acknowledging	knowledge	enlarger
particularly	altogether	able to	how
wonderful	responsible	acknowledge	to be

(b)

  (i) Notwithstanding-the very difficult commercial-conditions, we-had a satisfactory year of-trading. (**13**)

 (ii) Although-we-have to-be thankful for more trade this year, we-have nevertheless to-aim at enlarging our market in-the-months to-come. (**25**)

(iii) I-cannot-say that our January figures are particularly satisfactory but-we-shall do better before many-months have passed. (**20**)

(iv) She-is a wonderful typist. She takes responsibility very-well, and copes satisfactorily with any difficulties. (**16**)

 (v) They-are acknowledged to-be very influential and to-have more sources of information than-the rest. (**17**)

76

SECTION 21

2 PHRASES

I will consider, I shall contact, in control, at the conference, more than, lower than, higher than, as soon as, as soon as possible, this month, next month, it is not possible, out of, take off, set off, you have, who have, number of, there will not be, your requirements, we are arranging, we have been, at once, sales department, this committee, they will consider we are confident, very common.

3 DICTATION

(a) Easy
Dear Sirs, We hope to complete the contract for the / two computers this month, and we are arranging for our / commercial manager to visit our customers in January. As soon / as the contract is signed, we shall require all the / parts to be ready for dispatch within two weeks. Will / you please make a note of the likely dates for / shipping these parts which are given in the list attached / together with the names of ships and their sailing dates. / Yours truly, (**82**)

Dear Miss Jones, Will you please write and confirm that / the staff conference which was arranged for 10th December will / now take place on 14th January? I have had no / letter from you. Nevertheless, I have been told that one / was sent, but the post office states that a mail / bag was lost in a fire. It may be that / your communication to me was among the items lost. Information / has come to me from our salesmen that this is / the new arrangement. In the circumstances I will wait until / I hear officially from you before I make arrangements for / a committee meeting after the conference is over. Yours truly, / (**110**)

(b) Standard
It has been said that genius is one-tenth inspiration / and nine-tenths perspiration. What that really means is that / there is no substitute for hard work. True enough, luck / may be one of the conditions of success, but it / is also true that to achieve material success, your mental / attitude and your capacity for steady concentrated work play the / most considerable part. In a sense you may sometimes, as / Dr Samuel Smiles said in his famous book *Self Help*, / make your own good luck. Many people start out on / the long road to acquire high qualifications full of confidence / and energy. Yet after a few months all their energy / and enthusiasm seem to disappear, and the consequence is that / they give up because they did not recognise at the /

77

start that the road would be long and hard. Success / depends on continuous effort and the firm determination to grapple / with difficulties and conquer them. There is compensation in the / fact that if you are determined to succeed and battle / your way through the early difficulties, you find that the / work 'grows on you' and seems to become steadily easier / and more interesting. No doubt this is what Samuel Smiles / meant by making your own good luck. (**207**)

(c) Standard

We have just confirmed the contracts for office cleaning for / the next two years. One of the conditions of the / contracts is that all carpets shall be vacuum-cleaned twice / a week. This condition was inserted at the request of / the Staff Association. It would be convenient for the Office / Services Company Limited, who are doing the work, and it / would also contribute to keeping down the cost, if every / office floor were to be kept completely free of any / items except, of course, the furniture of the rooms. We / are confident that you will all do your best to / ensure that this is done, and we shall consult with / the Staff Association to seek a simple scheme to effect / it. (**121**)

An encyclopaedia is a fascinating book. The word is Greek / and it means 'all round knowledge'. Such works contain information / about the whole field of human knowledge, so the best / of them appear in many volumes. A very famous one / which is recognised as the most complete and comprehensive survey / of knowledge in existence has three parts. The first part, / the 'micro' part, has over 100,000 entries but / each one is limited to 750 words / or less. The 'macro' part has only 420 / articles but these cover over twenty-two / thousand pages and comprise twenty-eight million words. The third / part is an eight-hundred-page summary of all knowledge / and a supplement that appears every few years to keep / the encyclopaedia up to date. Scholars of 131 / nations contributed to produce this vast work. (**149**)

4 THEORY CHECKS

consume	comfort	discomfort	institute
contempt	compensate	uncontrolled	substitute
continent	combine	inconsistent	irritate
consent	command	recommendation	accommodation
conscious	commensurate	incognito	extradition

5 FREE DICTATION

It sometimes takes almost as long to get out of / an airport as it does to make the flight by / air. First you join a long line of people waiting / to pass through Immigration Control. Here they inspect your passport, / make sure that you have met all the conditions of / entry and consider whether you are a fit person to / be allowed into the country. Then you stand in a / packed crowd waiting for your baggage. Next you may have / to pass through an Exchange Control in which a long / form has to be filled in stating exactly what money / you are bringing into the country, and in what form / this money exists. Then you have one more hurdle to / jump and sometimes this is the worst of all. It / is called Customs, and here you may be unlucky enough / to have to open all your bags and then see / the contents that you have so neatly packed turned into / a jumble sale. At last, weary and distressed, you leave / the airport, perhaps recalling the old joke 'If you've time / to spare, then go by air!' (**186**)

The Pitman 2000
Dictionary of English
and Shorthand

Containing the shorthand outlines and meanings of over 75000 words, this invaluable work of reference includes a summary of the changes in the Pitman 2000 form of Pitman's Shorthand. American pronunciation and spelling is included with cross-referenced entries showing the differences.

216 × 138 mm/848 pages/Cased
ISBN 0 273 01618 0

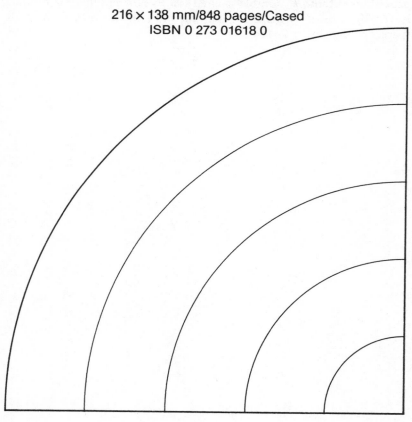

Pitman's Shorthand Speed Examination Practice No. 1

This book contains a selection of the shorthand examination material set by the RSA, the LCCI and ScotBEC during 1978. The material is written in Pitman 2000 Shorthand with a longhand key at the back of the book counted in tens for dictation.

● Speed range from 50 wpm to 120 wpm.

216 × 138 mm/128 pages/Paper
ISBN 0 273 01500 1

Pitman 2000 Shorthand Medical Words and Phrases Janice Kerr

An invaluable work of reference for those studying medical stenography. It contains a word list and a phrase list, and lists of drugs, tropical diseases and selected medical abbreviations. The vocalized shorthand outlines are intended as an aid to pronunciation and accurate transcription.

216 × 138 mm/96 pages/
Paper ISBN 0 273 01203 7

A Secretary's Guide to the Legal Office

A general guide to the typing of legal documents which then deals specifically with the documents encountered in each of the departments of a legal office — Probate, Conveyancing and Litigation — with short explanations of their purpose. Useful appendices having been included containing the Shorthand outlines for the words and phrases, legal abbreviations and exercises with keys.

A4/80 pages/Paper
ISBN 0 273 00704 1

Pitman 2000 Shorthand Phrase Book

Bryan Coombs

A valuable course in phrasing that is intended for use once the basic principles of Pitman 2000 Shorthand have been mastered. This book is designed to extend considerably the student's reading and writing skills. This is achieved by explanations and illustrations of the phrasing principles. Each chapter contains a phrasing drill of continuous material, a correspondence section and a long passage for reading and dictation. A key, counted in tens for dictation, is provided.

216 × 138mm/128 pages/Paper
ISBN 0 273 01802 7

Eight 1 ⅞ ips cassettes contain all the practice material from *Phrase Book* — all dictated first at 80 wpm and then at 100 wpm.

Pitman 2000 Shorthand Speedbuilder

Bryan Coombs

Following the style of the popular New Era title, this book retains the 'Skill of Shorthand Writing' and 'Correspondence' sections, reproducing them in Pitman 2000 Shorthand. The two versions will be invaluable in mixed speed classes of New Era and Pitman 2000 writers. Based on the principle that the faster students can read shorthand the faster they will be able to write it, the book is structured in such a way that the individual can measure progress by the use of timing columns.

216×138 mm/144 pages/Paper
ISBN 0 273 00879 X